Time and the Temple

Time and the Temple

God and Man

LUIGI GIUSSANI

Translated by Sofia Carozza

With the assistance of Laura Ferrario and Gregory Wolfe

TIME AND THE TEMPLE
God and Man

Copyright © 2026 Fraternità di comunione e liberazione. All rights reserved. Except for brief quotations in critical publications or reviews, no part of this book may be reproduced in any manner without prior written permission from the publisher. Write: Permissions, Slant Books, P.O. Box 60295, Seattle, WA 98160.

Slant Books
P.O. Box 60295
Seattle, WA 98160

www.slantbooks.org

Cataloguing-in-Publication data:

Names: Giussani, Luigi.

Title: Time and the temple / Luigi Giussani.

Description: Seattle, WA: Slant Books, 2026

Identifiers: ISBN 978-1-63982-215-7 (hardcover) | ISBN 978-1-63982-214-0 (paperback) | ISBN 978-1-63982-216-4 (ebook)

Subjects: LCSH: Vocation | Vocation--Christianity | Vocation, Ecclesiastical | Vocation (in religious orders, congregations, etc.)

Contents

Translator's Note | vii
Introduction | ix
1. God: The Temple and Time | 1
2. Recognizing Christ | 22
3. God and Man | 52
4. The Subject in Time and in the Temple: The I | 70
Appendix | 85
Notes | 94

Translator's Note

THIS VOLUME contains three meditations that Luigi Giussani gave during the Spiritual Exercises of the *Memores Domini* (a lay association of men and women living the evangelical counsels) in 1994 and 1995, and one given to the university members of Communion and Liberation in December 1994 ("Recognizing Christ").

The four meditations were originally given as speeches. Because Giussani spoke from a set of prepared points rather than a written script, the text includes digressions, interjections, and other features of spoken language. I have retained these elements to preserve his original voice and style. Giussani also employs repetition of words and phrases, sometimes with slight variations, to emphasize and bring out the complexity of their meaning. In such cases, I have occasionally used different English translations of the same Italian term to reflect its nuanced usage and preserve the richness of the original.

In this translation, I have rendered the Italian *l'uomo* as "the human person" to reflect the universal sense intended by the author. Where English grammar requires a gendered pronoun—even when the Italian may be neutral—I have alternated between masculine and feminine forms; these are meant to refer inclusively to all human persons.

Finally, I have added explanatory endnotes to provide context for names, events, and specific words, and have included scriptural citations not present in the original text.

Translator's Note

I am grateful to Laura Ferrario, Gregory Wolfe, and Paolo Carozza for helpful suggestions, and to Fr. Paolo Cumin FSCB for introducing me to this magnificent text.

Sofia Carozza
Solemnity of Christ the King

Introduction

THE FOUR TEXTS that make up this volume consist of meditations given between November 1994 and May 1995. However, their content echoes thoughts, reflections, and insights that stretch far back in time. I do not exaggerate in saying that I see them as a kind of brief, ideal synthesis of what I have sought to communicate in recent years to young people, as I have shared in their needs and expectations.

The theme of vocation is central in the experience of every Christian. I am not referring to a religious vocation in the strict sense—which is nevertheless discussed in these pages—but to what, for a Christian, constitutes life itself; life finds all its meaning in being a response to a call. God chose to come face-to-face with the human person by becoming a man, in order to communicate himself to the world and to people of every age. Herein lies all the originality of Christianity and its distinctiveness with respect to other religions: the relationship with the infinite is not fixed, imagined, or conceived by the person, but determined by the mysterious and real presence of God himself in human history.

In this regard there are three points that I would like to emphasize.

1. First, the method of the relationship between God and the person. God's involvement with human life always occurs through a point in time and space that is specific and carnal, a point at which the Mystery intervenes. It is the idea of a temple.

Introduction

It is a matter of recognizing the method God has chosen to make himself known to the human person, the method of his mysterious and real initiative to establish a relationship with the human person. And thus the one who, by grace, unexpectedly becomes aware of this initiative can choose to respond—looking to that new beginning, not of his own making, which has happened to him and which proves to correspond so profoundly to his needs and expectations.

Andrew and John came across that man, who dressed like everyone else, but was so different from the others: on that day and at that hour, something came into their lives that gave them a new birth, that made them different toward themselves and others. They followed him. The calling of every Christian, of every baptized person, is like the calling of the apostles: it does not depend on us, nor does it require any special conditions, but it happens through an encounter with an exceptional presence within a place and a time. The temple, in time.[1] This method has daily implications, in every moment. Nothing is useless anymore, and everything reveals an ultimate positivity.[2]

2. A new morality arises in those who thus begin to follow God's method, a new feeling of life: a feeling of seriousness, responsibility, creativity, and freedom which, little by little, tends to permeate the whole of life—both their own and that of others. It is a new morality that confronts the tragedy of the world; one that neither originates in, nor depends upon, laws that are discovered and grounded in analysis, but rather upon the fascination of an encounter. In the person, morality begins as the work of an other whom the person recognizes.

It is a new meaning of morality, flowing from the acceptance of that unforeseeable but real presence. This is what happened to Simon when he replied to Christ's questioning with, "Yes, you know that I love you" (John 21:16). Life, for the one who is called—that is, for the baptized—is thus the offering of every moment, gesture, word, and sorrow for the glory of Christ, that Christ may be recognized.

Introduction

And the glory of Christ is a term that refers to the present world, that concerns history; it does not take place in the life beyond, but in the here and now. Ultimately, then, vocation consists in recognizing Christ's ability to save the present moment of time. Conversely, this is what the modern age strives, in its most acute expressions, to deny.

3. This fruitfulness in time and space is the origin of a new people in history, which becomes the protagonist of history.

For the Christian, life is a response to a you who is present, a response more powerful than any effort and firmer than any achievable coherence. From this follows a new conception of oneself, which is renewed every day as an overcoming of the ways of the world and an appreciation of all that is good, true, and just in reality. Only one who is secure in the journey can value everything she encounters on the way, and every piece that she gathers becomes useful for building. This is why ecumenism is an authentically Christian concern: where one is certain about the supreme truth, about the face of Christ, by looking at him, everything one encounters reveals something good. Much more than an indifferent tolerance, ecumenism is love for the reverberation of truth found in anyone. It is a force for peace, the building of a human dwelling place, a home, that can be a refuge from even the most extreme despair. It means developing the potential of each one in relation to all persons; therefore, it always involves a clear judgment, even on one's companions on the way, so that the embrace might be unified, powerful, without anything left behind, and we might all walk together toward the heavenly kingdom "that fulfills every feast / for which the heart has longed" (Jacopone da Todi).[3]

1

God: The Temple and Time

THIS MORNING'S CONVERSATION is a dialogue that I want to establish between me and those of you who will make your profession tonight.[4] But, more profoundly—even though there is the risk that it will fall on deaf ears—this dialogue is to recall those who by God's gift have been called like yourselves and have already spent years upon years, many years, in the great possibility of those four walls of the house. Because of our spiritual dullness, which prevents us from understanding and perceiving, this time may have been passed amid distraction—which is nevertheless not a contradiction so radical as to constitute a betrayal, the word that is the exact opposite of profession.

"Profession" is affirming before the world; "betrayal" is denying before the world. "Before the world" is synonymous with "before God," because it is in the world that we know God, it is in the world that we walk toward God, it is in the world that we glorify Christ, it is in the world that we build Christ's kingdom. The world is not God, but it is the place of God: this world.

I would like what we say this morning to slowly begin to drip into your souls. At its origin, the soul is arid—of a dryness that thirsts—and bare, for it must be clothed with greenery, with freshness, with this "home" that we mentioned last night. We spoke of it as the piece of time and space, the piece of the world, the piece of history that interests you, that passes through and enters your being, precisely as the place where Christ is shown, is displayed as in an exhibition, is revealed as King of the Universe.

Now, what is the law of this house, which in ancient times was designated by the term dwelling or temple? A law is a description of a stable mechanism—a stable dynamism, as I used to say many years ago when I taught religion class. If something is alive, the dynamism of its life is described by a law; it indicates why the life grows, when it grows, and how much it grows.

A law. What is the dynamic law by which a house is a house? What is the dynamic law that governs the development of a house? Everything that God allows is for a development, for a life, for a history, for a destiny; from his hands everything emerges as a seed, as a promise. What is the dynamic law of a house's being and development? I hope the question is clear.

There is a book that was written to call humankind back to this very event, to the event of the whole organism that God has raised up so that it may be and remain in the world as the focal point and the goal of development, as the beginning and the end of everything. There is a book written to call humankind back to the event of this great organism whose law we seek—the generative law, the law that protects it from everything else and that makes it overcome all resistance—not taking away resistance but overcoming all resistance to bring its life to completion, to bring it to the day of righteousness, on the great day of Christ, the day of the Apocalypse. This book—it is clear—is the Bible. Indeed, the whole history of the Jewish people is a heralding of what was to happen to all humanity. Therefore, if one reads the history of the Jewish people with intelligence and humility—and with affection toward the mystery of Being, toward the mystery of the Father—one can easily observe these lines of development, these signs of its purpose. Saint Paul calls the history of the Jewish people "the great pedagogue," the great teacher that God created, formulated, aided, and destined to prepare humanity.[5]

Mind you, the way that the Jewish people prepared the world for the great Event—the pedagogy that it represents—applies more to us who have come later than to the people of that time, who did not know or recognize the significance of the Jewish people.[6] But God made the Jewish people with its history to be a pedagogy, to be an illuminating introduction to the nature of his involvement in the world, the nature of his involvement in history. This preparation was more for us than for those of that time. It was for everyone, but for those of that time it was like a glimmer in the darkness of the fog; for us it is the certainty of a serene day, a day where the light has already appeared and the sun has already traveled a long way—perhaps tracing its furrow within the space of our distraction, but nevertheless taking its path. In every moment you can redeem yourself and become aware of what you had never noticed before. And the word "house" is central to this realization, to this discovery, to this coming back of yours.

Well, the kingdom of Christ is like a great organism that has a law of being and development: a creative law of its beginning and, therefore, of its growth, until it reaches its destiny, its end, which is the total glory of Christ. We can call this law the law of *choice* or *election*.

For Christ to be all in all, for Christ to appear as all in all, for the glory of Christ to appear as the form and content of all things—"everything consists in him"—God, the Mystery, the Father, establishes a choice or election (Colossians 3:11; Colossians 1:17; John 1:3). Outside of this choice or election there can only be the reality of a crowd of wretches, beggars, who pick up the crumbs that fall from the children's table, exactly as the Canaanite woman said: "Even the dogs can feed on the crumbs that fall from the children's table" (Matthew 15:26).

Let us, therefore, trace the gradual enrichment of the objective content of this act of the Father, of the Mystery—this act we call choice, election, or calling. This is where it all begins. In fact, the great call, the great election, the great choice that God made for his plan in the world, is the call or election of Christ, the man who said, "What I see my Father doing, I always do. I do nothing but what I see my Father doing" (John 5:19). Reread, in this regard, chapters five, six, seven, and eight of Saint John's Gospel: "For this I was *sent*"—a choice, an election, a mission.

But, given this somewhat timid and oblique mention of the great call that gathers everything together and explains everything—the world, the life of each person and of all persons, of all peoples, and their movements and great migrations which have as their purpose, as Saint Paul says in the Areopagus of Athens, the search for God, that is, the search for God's plan for their existence, for their movement—let us leave it aside, that is, let us leave inscribed in the vault of heaven, which illuminates our steps, this mysterious and eternal election of Christ (Acts 17:26-28). Looking at history—at that story which bears the name of the month and the number of the year in which you and I were born, at the story of men, at the story of the world, the history-story—we see how this election or calling (which will later become what we will call mission) can be translated into a *list*, in the Greek sense of the word.[7]

First. The election of Our Lady, the choice of this young fifteen- or seventeen-year-old woman, that she might be and create the first dwelling place of God in the world, the first temple of the true and living God in the world; that she might be the first house of God in the world. Mary, you are the first house of God in the world, the first context, the first sphere, the first place in which everything that was there was of God, it belonged to God who came to live among us. All that you are—everything!—is for God, o dwelling place of his. There is no falsehood in you: "*Gratia plena.*"[8] The gift of God, the choice of God, has rendered you totally pure; indeed, more than rendered, it created you totally pure: "*Gratia plena.*" Therefore you are the most beautiful, because beauty is the splendor of the truth: the most beautiful!

And Nazareth, the house of Nazareth—which is the most striking thing on a pilgrimage to Palestine, out of everything it seems to me that this is the most striking: when one, from a little higher up, reads below, "The Word was made flesh here" (*Verbum caro hic factum est*).⁹ Here, here! "House"—the house of Nazareth is the first development of that house that is the womb of Mary, that is Mary herself. It is the first development of that personhood that was totally invested by Christ, which was totally *for* Christ: made, existing, alive, living, creative, full of grace, so that Christ might be recognized. The house of Nazareth is the first development of the house that is Our Lady.

And to think, friends, that three of us established a house in Nazareth this year!¹⁰ Is this not a sign that should stir us? Is it not a sign from God, through whom nothing happens in vain—least of all, something like this! Is it not a sign that he wants us all to wake up again, to reawaken all the *Memores Domini*, so that they might fulfill their mission in the world with more intelligence, with more affection, with more creativity, with more presence and not with the obscurity in which they drown most of their days? My friends, every phrase that seems like a recrimination from me today, with respect to you, is a reminder for you and a good wish for you! It is no longer, therefore, a mere reproach against your older companions and against myself.¹¹

Second. Please note that these points are pictures to meditate on, pieces of history to meditate on, to immerse oneself in, because what is alive today lives because it is a development of the event we have just recalled—which is therefore present. It is in relation to today like a root is to its plant. We have said that this reality of the house of Nazareth, this dwelling place of Nazareth, is a reality of time and space in which everything is for Christ. And who is the mediator, the demiurge, who makes what lies within his sphere to be wholly for Christ?¹² The human person, the person who has been called! This is the one who renews the world, who participates in the redemption of the world. This is the redeemer of the world in action, visibly: the one who has been called, the one who has been chosen, you who respond.

This reality of the house of Nazareth has spread throughout the whole world. It has spread: we can already say this! Saint Paul said, "it spreads" or "it is spreading" (Colossians 1:5-6; Romans

1:8). We can say that "it has spread" all over the world. We have two houses in Siberia, one in Moscow, two houses in New York, numerous houses in South America, in Kenya, and in Uganda.

This reality of the house of Nazareth has spread throughout the whole world through the choice of men and women who have been brought together into a single form, the Church. They have been made into a single reality: the body of Christ expanding through time and space, the one who was born of Our Lady, in his continuous birth within the world. It is the Church, the event that becomes present in the world and to the world, in all the moments, years, months, days, hours, and minutes of its history: the Church, the mysterious body of Christ.

This second point is followed by an important note. My friends, how much emotion, how much deep remorse, how much repentance, how much sorrow and how much joy, are consciously packed into every word I say! Through so many years of experience! Not only for me, but also for your older companions who have the responsibility of leading you, both personally and in your companionship. Every word I say is meant to be the last word on the things I speak of, on the time that I speak of, on the reality of the one who follows this path, on the world and on history. I mean each word to define your destiny, in this world and at the end of this world, when Christ will at last be all in all, and everyone will see him and say, "You all were right!" But already they are saying it, already many are saying it. You have perhaps heard them as well, and the letter I will read at the end (if there is enough time) will be one marvelous example among a thousand. What seem to you to be simply spoken phrases are in fact immense things, things to look at and to discover, to embrace, to love, to enter into as if taking a long journey (which is much better than all the tourist trips you dream of and even all the pilgrimages that replace, as a pretext, your touristic aspirations).

Here, then, is the important note. What is the force that enables this continuous development, the continuous development of that organism, the continuous remaining and renewing and multiplying of those dwelling places, of those houses? That is to say, what allows the expansion of the Church? What allows this continuous development is the Fact, the Guest of that house that was the womb of Our Lady. This Guest, the King of the Universe, "*cunctorum dominator alme*," the Guest of that house that was Our Lady's womb died on a cross so that this growth would come about, and rose from the dead so that everyone would understand that he is the King of the Universe.[13] And after a few weeks he ascended into heaven, which is to say, he descended into the depths where things are born, where everything is generated, where everything is created, instant by instant—everything. And from there he sends into the world his Spirit, who is the creator Spirit: "*Veni, creator Spiritus.*"[14] His Spirit like wind invests earthly reality, the reality of time and space, and, sweeping over it, transforms it continually. The culmination and the meaning of this creation of his Spirit is the expansion of his Church and the proliferation of his houses, his dwelling places. This is the history that brings meaning to the world; it is the story that brings meaning to the history of the world. And we are among those who have been called: there is no one here who has not been called—not even you, if you were just about to leave. This word of mine is worth more than any other: it is far more decisive, evaluative, productive, and creative than any word ever uttered by man or woman.

Third. The great dwelling place of the Church is incarnated—to use the term that comes to define the original Event[15] by which everything came into being and from which everything is born: the Word becomes incarnate in the womb of a young woman— the great dwelling place of the Church is incarnate, that is, is realized and becomes existent in *capillaries* (just as veins end in very thin capillaries), by which it becomes present in every particular environment, in every environment chosen by God's plan: Tibet is promised, but not yet chosen.[16]

The great dwelling place of the Church is incarnate, is realized in capillaries within each particular, chosen environment. And, above all, in houses, in dwelling places. Let us consider these houses, these dwelling places that function as the capillaries of the Church and that define, or express, the material of the environment in which one is, the substance of the people to which one belongs. These houses, or dwellings, can be of two kinds:

(a) The home of those who are called to make a family and thus (pay attention!) to shape the instrument—the family is an instrument—to shape the generative instrument from which emerges the subject of all historical action, the protagonist of God's plan, which is the human person. This is the normal vocation, without which history would end: the family, the root of the perennial development of history, the house of Jesus, dwelling place of the Son of Man.

(b) The monastery, etymologically the most meaningful word of all, because it derives from *monos*—alone, solitary. Indeed, humanity's relationship with God, with the Mystery, becomes consciousness, freedom, and love in the individual person: he becomes a new "I."[17] But "monastery" means many "I"s that are together. Even the example of the hermit has a temporariness that fails to make a law. All these *monoi*, in one way or another, express and testify to their being one with each other in the Church of God by coming together. Here, then, is the second word analogous to the word monastery: "convent" (which means coming together), or companionship, family, or house.

Monastery, convent, or house, according to the various modalities of the call: those who would go with Father Emmanuel[18] go to a convent, those who would go with Mother Rosy[19] go to a monastery, those who would go with Dario go to a house.

Monastery, convent, or house: made, created, built, generated by those who have been chosen to be living stones. Chosen for what? Chosen as a living stone to form, to generate an existence that can be experienced by all—which shows, by its very visible form, that God alone is. In the monastery, in the convent, or in the houses, these living stones, those who have been called and chosen, have been called to show by the very visible forms of their lives that he alone is. You who make profession today are called to demonstrate by the visible form of your life—simply by the visible form of your life—that Christ is the King of the universe: "*Christe, cunctorum dominator alme*," "*omnia in ipso constant*": everything consists in him, from him (Colossians 1:17).

A monastery, convent, or house, therefore, is that place created so that those who live there will cry out before everything, at every moment—because their whole life is made for this—that Christ is the only thing that makes life worth living, that Christ is the only thing that makes it worthwhile for the world to exist. But this is as true as two plus two equals four: that Christ is the only thing that makes it worthwhile for the world to exist, that Christ is the only thing that makes it worthwhile for history to be carried out.

What about you? Have you heard those older than you in the house, have you heard them shouting this out in front of everyone, all the time? "They would be crazy, they would be crazy!" you are thinking. But they would not be crazy: they are crazy if they remain unaware, if they are not aware of this fact. For their whole life is made up of this. That they cry out in front of everyone at every moment that Christ is the only reason life is worth living: this is the very form of their life. It is the very form of their life, regardless—I will say it twice more—regardless even of the integrity with which they live. Almost in spite of themselves.

This is the *objective value* of the vocation: the *form* of their life competes in the world for Christ, fights in the world for Christ. The very form of their life! Therefore, when they made their profession, they made a grand gesture—the greatest gesture of their existence. If their days, their instants, all their moments, their steps, if their whole path does not follow through on this dedication, if something is missing, if it fails—which is the concept of "sin"—if it falls short of this dedication, they struggle all the same by virtue of the objective form of their life: it is a life consecrated to Jesus. It is a life that as a form cries out, "Jesus is everything." They shout this in front of everyone who sees them, everyone who comes across them, everyone who hears them, everyone who looks at them.

Time and the Temple

In other words, those who live in the monastery, the convent, or the house have been called to be *prophets*. It is prophecy in the world, because to be prophets means to cry out before everyone (*pro-femi*), to cry out before everyone that Christ is everything.[20] And to say that "Christ is everything" is to be a prophet of the future, because if Christ is everything, what will become of your betrayals of today and yesterday? Therefore, prophecy tends to change the life of today so that the hell of tomorrow, the lack of meaning of tomorrow, does not come about.

Prophets. Like Moses, about whom you will read in the third chapter of Exodus, the moment when God called him and he immediately responded, "But who am I to go and do this? Who am I to do this in the world?" In the world: for it has to do with the history of the world. And your protagonism is such that without it, something would be lost from the history of the world—from the history of the world! Or like Isaiah, who responded, "Here I am, send me" with the spontaneity, the liveliness, the richness, the splendor of an adolescent (Isaiah 6:8). Or Jeremiah in chapter twenty, who represents well your elderly and even not-so-elderly companions, who will represent perhaps you yourselves in a few months, if you do not beg for liveliness every day, if you do not brandish it every morning when you get out of bed, if you do not oppose it to every temptation. If, on the other hand, you do beg for liveliness, it enters into the damage done by your errors, digging into it to restore life to your flesh; their life will be like fresh grass (Isaiah 66:14). Jeremiah said, "When did I ever enter into this frame of mind! Why, who called me? I almost curse the day my mother gave birth to me! Look at what a battle I got into! What a continuous choice I must make! What a renunciation!" (Jeremiah 20). And it seems to be such: when you discover, sooner or later, that what seems to be a renunciation is not a renunciation, but a deeper possession, then you will not be ashamed of yourself. You will rather be in awe of the Most High, you will be in awe of Christ, and you will feel inundated with tenderness toward your body, your heart, and your spirit. With a tenderness that does not exist around you—except as a cover for instinct, as a formula for instinctiveness. Tenderness is the greatness of a heart that is moved, of an eye wide open to the infinite. It is the expansion of the heart that embraces the infinite, that embraces everything. "Christ is all in all": this is a formula that becomes in time always more and more of an experience—increasingly an experience!

You are a prophet, you who make the profession today, "to guide our feet—the feet of us poor men and women—into the way of peace" (Luke 1:56-69). You alone will be able to truly, consciously wish, you alone will know how to wish your fellow men and women who pass you by, who stand with you on the streetcar, who meet you on the street, who oppose you or favor you or are indifferent to you, you alone will be able to wish them: "*Sint dies laeti placidaeque noctes*" [May days be glad and nights serene], according to the expression of the *Christe cunctorum dominator alme* (which could be a hymn by Saint Ambrose, both the words and the music.[21] His supreme way of preaching, of evangelizing, was song: words and music. And this hymn could have been written by Saint Ambrose because it is a great work, a great poem, grandiose and great). To all people we would like to bring this wish: "*Sint dies laeti placidaeque noctes.*" *Noctes placidae*: placid, at peace, not subverted by the poison of temptation, by the threat of failure, by the torment of fear over what is to come. *Dies laeti*, glad as a sunny day, even if the day were cold: but it is burning, like the March day described by Maria Barbara Tosatti in her poems.[22] Well then, prophecy is this.

Fourth. Those called to virginity are the figure of a prophet, about whom I have already shared some reflections just now.

Now, the figure of a virgin is the figure of a prophet. The figure of a virgin is the figure of a prophet by nature: don't worry about being one, you are one; if you make your profession, you are one; if you decide to be Christ's in virginity, you are a prophet. Don't consider prophecy except to become aware of what you are—not to describe a goal at which to arrive. Those called to virginity are the figure of a prophet.

Time and the Temple

This figure of a prophet, or the figure of a virgin, is the miracle of miracles. How do people recognize Christ, that Christ is God? What makes them begin to tremble, to doubt, and to say, "But you, where do you come from? Who are you?"—even though they knew everything about Jesus, he was enrolled in the registry of Bethlehem, they knew all the details of his home because they had been there so many times: by miracles (Luke 8:22-25; John 10:24). The prophet and the virgin are the miracle of miracles.

The miracle, in fact, as you will see in *Why the Church* if you haven't already studied it (and if you have already read those pages on miracles and don't remember them you are fools), the miracle is an event that necessarily recalls God.[23] Necessarily: it is an event whereby one is compelled to recall God. Even if he doesn't believe—and even if he will say "no" again later—he is obliged to think of God. The text distinguishes three cases, three levels of miracles.

The first level is creation, as Saint Paul says to the Romans: in looking at creation, all people understand that there is something other (Romans 1:19-20). The second level is a miracle as an emergent fact in my life, in my existence, through which God wants to call me, wants to change me, invites me to become different, saying, "I am favorable to you. You are mine and I am favorable to you. Why are you afraid?" Or rather, "Why do you betray me?" In this second sense a miracle is an event in my life that has forced me to think about God, that forces me to think about God. A miracle, in the broadest sense, is an extraordinary occurrence that compelled me to invoke Jesus and, as I remember it, compels me again to think of Jesus and I have no other explanation. All my friends, everyone who loves me, my neighbors, also understood it with me; and the neighbors that I have just told also understand; if they are not superficial, they too are struck—less than I am, but they are nonetheless affected. Instead, the third level is when an event is so obvious, when it calls out to God with such an objective greatness and force—such an absence of "explainability" in other terms—that it is made manifest to the whole world, to people of every age and even to the scientists of every age, as are certain

God: The Temple and Time

miracles at Lourdes or Fatima. But the Church of Jesus, the house of Jesus—and analogously our own homes—never goes through a year without experiencing the presence of these great miracles.

Still, why do those called to virginity represent the miracle of miracles? Because there is no greater miracle than one who dedicates all of life to Christ, sacrificing natural instincts and tendencies that God placed within her, which she passes through and overcomes by giving her life to Christ. "What a beautiful girl you are, but are you married already?" he says with some hope. "No." "Ah!" "But I am not going to get married." "What! Why?" "Because Jesus Christ is greater than all: he makes me love everyone, he makes me feel loved like no one else could, he makes me value everything—even you, my friend." And he goes away a little ... let's say with his tail between his legs. There is no greater miracle: it is the human miracle par excellence, in which the human person becomes a factor in the miracle, the subject and object of the miracle itself. And then, that man sees this girl all day long in the office. So maybe he gives it a try anyway. And here, "*si parrà sua nobilitate*," here the nobility of the girl is put to the test, that is, her fidelity.[24] The vocation that she told him about earlier is an event whose explanation necessarily says "God" or "Jesus"; and he, seeing it, must keep thinking of Jesus or God, even though—full of anger—he wants to overturn the matter.

For this figure, however, to fulfill its prophetic calling—for you, my friend, to fulfill your prophetic calling—a few things are needed:

1. She must live the faith more than others. (I hope that you review what faith means and how faith is born in *Is It Possible to Live This Way?*, which is the account of a whole year of dialogue with the first-year novices.[25]) Faith is affirming a Presence whose origin cannot be seen, whose consistency cannot be seen. One sees only the endpoints of its gestures, certain facts, certain results—the endpoints of its gestures.

Let us return to the book of Exodus, to the second chapter. Moses was a murderer: he was called to lead his people. You are a prophet because you are called to virginity, you are a prophet because you are a virgin, even if you had your days that were riddled with errors.

This is more or less the line of reasoning that the Old Testament writers follow, especially in the Psalms, when they say: Lord, be faithful. You are faithful to your covenant. Because of your name, that is, for the dignity of your plan, for your dignity that is revealed in your design, for your dignity as the one triumphant, as victor, as ruler over all, as King of the universe, even if I make a mistake—even if I have made a mistake—do not abandon me. Chastise me for what I have done, but do not break your covenant. Keep me on the path.

Therefore, every moment is good. Every moment is good because every moment is an occasion for beginning again, for pain and for beginning again. And the past becomes a source of richness for the present; insofar as it was a mistake, it is as if the past did not exist. As Oscar Milosz makes Miguel Mañara say: "All these things never existed. He alone is."[26] This is the only strength, the only source of fullness and joy for any person on earth: "He alone is."

2. She must be able to give the reason for her faith more than others. Precisely because her calling makes her capable of giving more of a reason, of describing more broadly and densely the effects of God's presence in life, the changing of life: "He is, if he works," "he is, if he changes," "he is, when he changes," one of you told me.[27] He is, because he changes—an even better formulation. One is a sinner all life long and yet all of life changes: what an infinite thing!

3. She must—pay attention to these words!—make the faith the form of her actions: whether she eats or drinks, whether she keeps watch or sleeps, whether she lives or dies (1 Corinthians 10:31; 1 Thessalonians 5:10; Romans 14:8). She must make the faith the form of her actions, so that gradually every action is made perfect by the end that she pursues, by the consciousness that she follows, as perfect as the ultimate meaning of history: Jesus, the man Jesus, God.

God: The Temple and Time

Now, note this fourth point (if you bear with me, I will finish in twenty minutes; however, you who make the profession of faith will not find anything or anyone who will tell you the truth about yourselves and your life with as much passion and awareness as you hear it from those who are responsible for the *Memores Domini*). If charity is a gift of self, born from a heart that is moved, if charity is loving the other through this moved self-giving (I hope you will discover this in the book I mentioned earlier),[28] if charity is affirming the other in his or her destiny—a gift of self to the other and love of the destiny of the other, therefore, a gift of me to the other, my life as service of the other, service of the path of the other, and continual affirmation of the destiny that awaits him or her as light and peace ("to guide our feet into the way of peace")—then there is no greater charity than virginity (Luke 1:79).

There is no greater charity than virginity (Mother Teresa of Calcutta, if she were here, would be pounding her fist on the table saying, "Yes, it is true!"). For in virginity, I give myself to the other, even to the most wretched one who approaches me—but the difference between wretched and not wretched no longer matters. I give myself for the sake of the other person's path, continually affirming, continually reminding him, of the destiny for which he is made: Jesus—continually reminding him of Jesus. Either one is an impostor or, by reminding the other, one also reminds oneself.

Thus virginity is the fulfillment of the moral law for each person, who is called to implement it according to one or the other type of vocation. Virginity is the culmination of the moral law for those who have the other vocation, too. That Jesus is everything—"*cunctorum dominator alme*"—that he is the source of peace and joy in life, of stability and constructiveness, is as true for my father and my mother as for me. But I am called by the very form of my life to recall my father and mother to this fact. Therefore our parents, when they see us—your parents, when they see you—change: they change their gaze on you. Even if they remain irritated and opposed to what you do, they are still struck by what you do.

Virginity is the pinnacle of the moral law for each person, who is called to implement it according to one or another kind of vocation, since life as a vocation means that life is a calling to a certain way of collaborating in the history of the universe. Life is a call to collaborate in the history of the universe, that is, in the reign of Christ: willingly or unwillingly, consciously or unconsciously.

Thus we can also understand the immediate, visible, sensorially perceptible difference between the two paths: virginity is the more significant one. That a person is a father or mother is right, it is understandable in natural terms. But virginity is more meaningful. A father and mother who try to live virginity in their relationship—in fact, it is referred to as marital chastity—this is more significant even than their being father and mother. They are father and mother in Christ's name: it is an intention they give to themselves, to everything that they do. But if this reaches a purity in their relations with one another, then it truly becomes more meaningful.

Virginity is more meaningful and resounds with immediacy. The other road is troubled by the flesh, Saint Paul said: "You will have tribulation in the flesh, I would like you to avoid it" (1 Corinthians 7:28). The tribulation of the flesh is more of an impediment. That is why I spoke—to the scandal of many—of "restraint": the flesh becomes restraint.[29] As in the *Noli me tangere* of Fra Angelico, in that detail depicting Mary Magdalene who reaches out to Jesus; as soon as she sees him, that is, as soon as she realizes that the one she previously thought was the gardener is Jesus, she rushes toward him.[30] And Jesus stops her with his hand. One sees the two hands of the Magdalene and the hand of Jesus that restrains—which is the image that we have always given of virginal possession, which tends toward totality.[31] But as long as this tending toward totality is within a hair's breadth of the other's face, then one truly possesses, much more than even if one were to venture upon the face itself: by venturing upon the other's face, the hand becomes more like an animal's paw. The other path will have tribulation in the flesh, that is, it will have as an eternal contradiction that thirst for possession that is the material substance of a non-virginal relationship (1 Corinthians 7:28).

God: The Temple and Time

Fifth. The moment of profession sets the date when Christ, in his Church, places before all the believing and unbelieving people those whom he has called, those whom he has chosen to be sent throughout the world. You are not sent along a particular street, or to your own town: you are chosen to be sent into the whole world (the best part comes now!) to be, by the profession of your life—you should write this freely on your identity card—not the father or mother of a family, not an administrator or an architect, not an executive or a worker: your profession of life will be the prophetic proclamation of all these things we have said. With the very form of your life, the form, that is, of one who does not marry in order to break through to that phenomenon of total espousal with everyone and with everything, that is the promise of the reality of Christ as it appears to the eye and heart of believers.

Profession of life: not father and mother of a family, administrator or architect, executive or worker, but virginity. "What do you do?" "The form of my life is a prophetic proclamation," a prophetic proclamation of all these things.

So, how does this work, this profession, come about? The work involved in this profession gives no reprieve to any action; every action is an offering-to (every true action). God, hasten to fulfill the promise you made by giving me this vocation. This "hasten" will be repeated for ten years, twenty years, fifty years, seventy years—a hundred years if God lets you have them—and in the end each one who has remained faithful on the road will experience the promise, despite all the tribulations of the flesh which otherwise remain in him as a completely deceitful claim. The tribulations of the flesh remain, though not like they do on the other road, because in marriage the claim to possession is the constant matter of the vocation, the law and material content of the vocation itself.

Sixth. There is a significant difference between the Old and New Testaments. In the Old Testament the prophet could still be doubtful in responding to God, not in the sense of a doubt accompanying the dynamic of adhering to him (we all have that), but as an initial rejection of the vocation: "I am not able, who am

I to be called? But I have committed. . . ." There is no trace of any of these things, of any of these objections, in the "yes" that Simon says to Jesus in the twenty-first chapter of Saint John's Gospel; he could very well have voiced these objections, but instead, there is no trace of them. "Do you love me?" "Yes. Yes, you know that I love you." In the New Testament the prophet says "yes" to an event that is present. Just as Christ was not uncertain between yes and no: his life was a yes to the Father (2 Corinthians 1:19-20).

It is as if in the Old Testament the person were bent on serving God, on serving Yahweh. In the New Testament the person loves a Presence. "Simon, do you love me?" "Yes" (John 21:15). And the seconds that passed between Jesus's question and Simon's "yes" were not a doubt or an uncertainty: it was the time it took to go through all his memories, to wipe out all his memories in order to say "yes," which was the true expression of his heart.

The choice of virginity is a call to say "yes" ultimately and even independently of one's own mistakes. The choice of virginity is a call to say "yes": ultimately this "yes" is independent even of one's mistakes, like Simon's "yes," which we will never remember often enough—every day we must conjure up again that scene, for it happens in us!

One can live this unavoidability that the choice of virginity entails, one can live this irresistibility of the "yes" with forgetfulness, with reserve, with reticence, even with skepticism, condemning ourselves thus to the elimination of joy. Or one can live, even bouncing along with the rhythm of a sine wave—up and down, up and down—but with intensity of memory, continually beginning to tend toward him again, thus granting the relationship you establish with the whole of reality (with your father, your mother, your siblings, your friends, your childhood companion) the creativity of making reality be a collaborator in your joy, bending reality itself to collaborate in your own joy. Reality becomes entirely collaborative in one's own joy. Even evil becomes cooperative in one's own joy: "*omnia cooperantur in bonum,*" everything works together for good (Romans 8:28). And Saint Augustine adds "*etiam mala*"; even our evil is compelled to become a collaborator in our joy.[32] It

God: The Temple and Time

is in this joy that the formula of creation, the glory of the Father, is fully realized. The formula of creation is *"omnis creatura bona,"* every creature is a source of joy (Genesis 1:31). Even death: *"cupio dissolvi,"* I want to die and be with Christ, Saint Paul says, because this is in fact how death is destroyed (Philippians 1:21-23). Virginity is against death. Death is destroyed and Christ reigns completely: *"Christe, cunctorum dominator alme."*

T.S. Eliot, in the play *The Family Reunion*, says, "In a world of fugitives / The person taking the opposite direction / Will appear to run away."[33] This is the virgin in the world of today: the one who is interested in the nature of things and the destiny of things, for the human person, for the joy of the person and for the glory of the truth that is Christ. Therefore, keen admiration for the little flowers of the field, for the leaf of a tree, for pine needles and the number of pine needles that are on the ground—these things do not escape such a one. ("I wonder, Mama, how does God know the number of all the pine needles that are on the ground?" It was a fair question, which I asked my mother when I was five years old). Everything interests the virgin, everything; there is nothing that escapes his observation, and the more that he grows the more he becomes childlike in observing everything. The child, in his curiosity, leaves no space without an attempt to grasp every aspect, even the smallest, of the thing he has in hand.

"In a world of fugitives / The person taking the opposite direction / Will appear to run away." Ours is not a renunciation of the world: it is the beginning of a journey toward possessing the whole world, so that we may be protagonists of the coming of the kingdom of Christ.

I would like to read, in conclusion, the letter I mentioned earlier.

"Dear Fr. Giussani . . ." I did not know this young man, nor did he know me. Think of the middleman, the person who served as middleman, because somehow—I don't know if he was married or unmarried—he was someone who lived virginity before the eyes of this dying man; two days after he wrote me this letter he died. He was sick with AIDS.

Time and the Temple

Dear Fr. Giussani, I write to you calling you "dear" even though I do not know you,[34] I have never seen you nor heard you speak. But to tell you the truth, I can say that I do know you in that—if I have understood anything of *The Religious Sense*[35] and of what Ziba[36] tells me—I know you by faith and, I now add, thanks to the faith [there, the middleman was therefore one called to virginity]. I am just writing to say thank you. Thank you for having given a meaning to this arid life of mine: I am a high school classmate of Ziba's, with whom I have always maintained a friendly relationship since, though I did not share his position, I was always struck by his humanity, his selfless availability. Of this troubled life I think I have reached the end of the line, carried by that train called AIDS that leaves no respite for anyone. Now saying this does not make me afraid anymore. Ziba always used to tell me that the important thing in life is to have a true interest and to follow it. I pursued this interest many times, but it was never the true one. Now I have seen the true one, I see him, I have met him, and I am beginning to know him, to call him by name: his name is Christ. I don't even know what that means or how I can say these things, but when I see the face of my friend or read *The Religious Sense* that is keeping me company, and I think of you or the things Ziba tells me about you, everything seems clearer—everything, even my evil and my pain. My life, which had been flattened and made barren, made like a smooth stone where everything runs off like water, receives a jolt of meaning and significance that sweeps away the wicked thoughts and sorrows. Or rather, it embraces them and makes them true, rendering my grubby and putrid body a sign of his presence. Thank you, Don Giussani, because you have communicated this faith—or, as you call it, this Event—to me. Now I feel at peace, free and at peace. When Ziba used to recite the Angelus in front of me who blasphemed to his face, I hated him and told him he was a coward because the only thing he knew how to do was to say those stupid prayers in front of me. Now, when I stutteringly try to say it with him, I realize that the coward was me because I couldn't even see an inch from my nose the truth that

God: The Temple and Time

was in front of me. Thank you, Don Giussani, is the only thing that a man like me can say to you. Thank you because in my tears I can say that dying like this now has a meaning. Not because it is more beautiful—I have a great fear of dying—but because now I know that there is someone who loves me and that I too can perhaps be saved and that I too can pray that my fellow patients might encounter and see as I have seen and encountered. So I feel useful—just think, only by using my voice I feel useful, with the only thing that I can still use well I can be useful. I who have thrown away my life can do good by simply saying the Angelus. It is striking, but even if it were an illusion this is too human and too reasonable, as you say in *The Religious Sense*, not to be true. Ziba attached to my bed the phrase of Saint Thomas: 'Man's life consists in the affection which principally sustains him and in which he finds his greatest satisfaction.'[37] I think my greatest satisfaction is to have known you by writing this letter to you, but the still greater one is that in God's mercy, if he wills it, I will know you there where everything will be new, good, and true. New, good, and true like the friendship that you have brought into the lives of many people and of which I can say, "I was there, too." I too in this wretched life have seen and participated in this new, good, and true event. Pray for me, I will continue to feel useful for the time I have left by praying for you and for the movement. I embrace you. Andrea.[38]

2

Recognizing Christ

THIS MORNING'S MEDITATION ended with Kafka's evocative phrase: "There is a goal, but no way."[39] It is undeniable that there is an unknown (the geographers of antiquity drew an analogy of this unknown with the famous expression *terra incognita* with which they marked the edge of their great map).[40] At the margins of reality that the eye embraces, that the heart feels, that the mind imagines, there is an unknown. Everyone feels it. Everyone has always felt it. In every age, people have felt it so strongly that their imaginations have given it a form. In every age, people have sought, through their speculations or fantasies, to imagine, to gaze on the face of this unknown. Tacitus, in his work *Germania*, described the religious feeling that defined the ancient Teutons[41] with these words: "*secretum illud quod sola reverentia vident, hoc deum appellant*"[42] (that mysterious thing they intuited in fear and trembling, this they called God). All people of every age, whatever image they make of the mystery, *hoc deum appellant*, call "God" this unknown one they look upon—many with indifference but also many with passion. Undoubtedly, among the passionate ones were those three hundred who walked in procession with Cardinal Martini from Saint Charles to the Cathedral of Milan.[43] Three hundred representatives of different religions! And what is a single, most basic term we could use for what they intended to express and honor by their participation in the great initiative of the Cardinal of Milan? A *secretum illud*, something mysterious, *terra incognita*, something unknowable—unknowable!

I would like to recall now a comparison found in *At the Origin of the Christian Claim*.[44] Imagine the human world, human history, as a vast plain and, in this vast plain, an immense throng of firms, of construction companies, that are particularly skilled at building roads and bridges. Each of them in their corners, from their corners, try to build a bridge connecting the point where they are, the ephemeral moment in which they live, to the star-studded sky, to use Victor Hugo's image in his beautiful poem from *Les Contemplations* entitled "Le Pont" ["The Bridge"].[45] Hugo imagines someone sitting on the beach at night, on a starry night, a man gazing up and staring at the largest and seemingly closest star. He thinks of the thousands and thousands of arches that would need to be erected to build such a bridge, a bridge that is never completely defined, never fully usable.

Imagine, then, this vast plain, all crowded with the attempts of groups large and small, or even of loners, as in Victor Hugo's image—each one carrying out the design he or she has imagined or dreamed up. Suddenly a powerful voice is heard in the vast plain, saying, "Stop! Everyone stop!" And all the workers, the engineers, the architects suspend their work and look in the direction from which the voice came: it is a man, who raises his arm and goes on, "You are great men, you are noble in your endeavor, but this effort of yours, though great and noble, is nevertheless a sad one. This is why many give up on it and think no more about it and become indifferent. It is great but sad, because it never accomplishes its goal, it never succeeds in reaching the end. You are incapable of it because you are powerless with respect to this goal. There is an unbridgeable disproportion between you and the farthest star of the sky, between you and God. You cannot imagine the mystery. Now leave your laborious and thankless work and follow me: I will build you this bridge, or rather, *I am* this bridge! Because I am the way, the truth, the life!" (John 14:6).

Time and the Temple

You cannot understand the serious intellectual value of these things unless you become one with them, unless you try to identify with them in your heart. Imagine, then, that on the sand dunes by the sea you see a huddle of people from the neighboring village listening to one of them speaking, to someone in the middle of the group who is speaking. You pass by them to go to the beach where you are heading; you pass close by, and as you pass by and look curiously, you hear the man standing in the middle say, "I am the way, the truth, the life! I am the way, the truth. . . .": the way that cannot be known, the way of which Kafka spoke: "I am the way, the truth, the life." Picture it, make an effort of the imagination, of fantasy: what would you do, what would you say? However skeptical you may be, you cannot but help but prick up your ears, attracted by something coming from that direction, and, at the very least, you look with utmost curiosity at that man who is either crazy or is telling the truth: *tertium non datur*,[46] either he is crazy or it is true. In fact, it is so true that only one man, only one, has ever said this phrase in the entire history of the world—of the world! A man amid a small group of people, often amid a small group but often amid a large crowd, too.

So, everyone in the great plain halts their work and pays attention to this voice, and he continually repeats the same words. Who were the first to be annoyed by this matter? The engineers, the architects, and the owners of the various construction companies, who said almost immediately, "Come on, come on, guys, get to work! Workers, back to your jobs! That guy is just a braggart!" He was a radical, trenchant alternative to their project, to their creativity, to their profit, to their power, to their name, to their very selves. He was the alternative to their own self. After the engineers, architects, and bosses, so also the workers—beginning to laugh a little—dragged their eyes away from the man more reluctantly, talking about him for a bit, making fun of him or saying, "Who knows, who knows who he is, could he be crazy?" Some of them, however, did not. Some heard an accent they had never heard before, and they did not respond to the engineer, architect, or company boss who said to them, "Come on, quickly, what are

Recognizing Christ

you doing here, why are you still stopping to look over there?" They kept looking at the man. And he came forward. Or rather, they went up to him. Out of 120 million people, there were twelve of them. But it happened: this is a historical fact.

What Kafka says ("there is no way") is not historically true. Paradoxically, one might say that it is true theoretically, but it is not true historically. The mystery cannot be known! This is true theoretically. But if the mystery knocks at your door. . . . "He who opens the door to me, I will enter his house and dine with him" are words we read in the Bible, they are the words of God in the Bible (Revelation 3:20). And it is a fact that happened.

The first chapter of the Gospel of Saint John, which is the first page in literature that speaks about it, besides making the general announcement—"The Word was made flesh," that of which all reality is made became man—contains the memories of those who followed him immediately, who resisted the urgings of the engineers and architects. On a sheet of paper, one of them jotted down his first impressions and the features of the first moment in which the fact occurred. Indeed, the first chapter of the Gospel of Saint John contains a series of notes that are just that—notes from memory. One of the two men, having grown old, reads the remaining notes from his memory. For memory has its own law. Memory does not follow a law of continuity without gaps, as for example in works of fantasy or imagination. Memory literally "takes notes," as we are doing now: a note, a line, a point, and this point covers many things, such that the second phrase begins from the many things that were assumed in the first point. Things are often supposed rather than stated, and some are only stated as landmarks. As a result, in my seventies I am rereading this passage for the thousandth time, and without any hint of fatigue. I challenge you to imagine anything in history that is more serious, more weighty, in the sense of *pondus*, greater, charged with more of a challenge to human existence in its apparent fragility, more pregnant with consequences than this fact that happened.[47]

Time and the Temple

"The next day John was there again with two of his disciples, and fixing his gaze on Jesus as he walked by, he said..."(John 1:35). Imagine the scene, then. After a hundred and fifty years of waiting, the Hebrew people—who, throughout their whole history, for two millennia, had always had some prophet, someone recognized by everyone as a prophet—finally had a prophet again: his name was John the Baptist. Other writings from antiquity also mention him; he is historically documented, therefore. Everyone—rich and poor, publicans and Pharisees, friends and opponents—went to hear him speak and to see the way he lived, beyond the Jordan, in the desert land of locusts and wild grasses. He always had a huddle of people around him. Among those people that day were also two who had come for the first time and were from, we would say, the country—they were actually from the lake, which was quite far away and out of the loop of the highly developed cities. They were there like two villagers coming to the city for the first time, bewildered, looking wide-eyed at everything around them and especially at John. They were there with their mouths open and their eyes gaping, looking at him and listening to him very attentively. Suddenly one of the group, a young man, leaves, taking the path along the river heading north. And John the Baptist, fixing his gaze on him, immediately cries out, "Behold the Lamb of God, behold him who takes away the sins of the world!" But the people did not move; they were used to hearing the prophet occasionally express himself in strange, unintelligible phrases, seemingly unrelated and out of context, so most of those present took no notice. The two who had come for the first time and were hanging on John's every word, watching his eyes, looking wherever he turned his gaze, saw that he was staring at that man who was leaving, and they set out after him. They followed him from a distance, timid and ashamed, but also strangely, profoundly, obscurely awestruck and intrigued. "The two disciples heard him say this, and followed Jesus. Jesus turned and saw them following him, and he said to them, 'What are you looking for?' They replied, 'Rabbi, where are you staying?' He said to them, 'Come and see.'"

This is the formula, *the* Christian formula. This is the Christian method: "Come and see." "So they went and saw where he was staying, and they stayed with him all that day. It was about four o'clock in the afternoon." It doesn't specify when they left, when they followed him. The whole passage and the following one too are made up of notes, as I said before; the sentences end at a point that takes for granted that we already know many things. For example, "It was about four o'clock in the afternoon." Does this refer to when they left, or when they arrived? Who knows? In any case, it was four o'clock in the afternoon. One of the two who had heard the words of John the Baptist and followed Jesus was named Andrew, and he was Simon Peter's brother. Indeed, the first person he met was his brother Simon, who was returning from the beach—he was either coming back from fishing or from mending his fishing nets—and he said to him, "We have found the Messiah." John doesn't narrate anything, doesn't quote anybody, doesn't offer any documentation. It is common knowledge, it is clear, these are notes about things that everyone knows! Few pages can be read that are so lifelike, so straightforwardly true, where not a single word has been added to pure recollection.

How could Andrew say, "We have found the Messiah"? Jesus, in speaking to them, must have used this word, which was part of their vocabulary, because saying that this man was the Messiah, asserting it so emphatically right away, would have been impossible. It shows that staying there for hours and hours listening to that man, seeing him, watching him speak—who could speak like that? Who had ever spoken like that? Who had ever said such things? Unheard of! No one had ever seen anyone like that!—slowly within their hearts grew the phrase, "If I don't believe this man I will no longer believe anyone, not even my own eyes." Not that they said it, not that they thought it; they felt rather than thought it. That man must therefore have said, among other things, that he was the one who was to come, the Messiah. But it was so obvious in the face of the exceptionality of the announcement that they came away with that statement as if it were something simple—and it was simple!—as if it were something easy to understand.

"And Andrew brought Simon to Jesus, who looked at him and said, 'You are Simon, son of John. You shall be called Cephas' (which means 'rock')." The Jews used to change someone's name either to indicate his or her character or to commemorate some event that had happened. So, imagine Simon going with his brother, full of curiosity and a bit of fear, and staring at the man to whom his brother has led him. The man is also looking back at him from a distance. Think of the way he looked at Simon, to the point of understanding his character down to the marrow of his bones: "You will be called Rock." Imagine one who feels he is being looked at in such a way by someone new, by a complete stranger; imagine one who feels he is grasped in the depths of his being. "The next day Jesus decided to depart for Galilee...." The rest you will read for yourselves. It is half a page just like this, made up of brief references and points that take for granted that everyone knew everything that had happened, that it was obvious to everyone.

"There is a goal, but no way." No! A man who said, "I am the way" is a historical fact that happened, the first description of which is in this half page I started reading. And every one of us knows that it happened. Nothing has every happened in this world that was as unthinkable and exceptional as the man of whom we are speaking: Jesus of Nazareth.

But those two, the first two, John and Andrew—Andrew was most likely married with children—how were they won over so quickly and able to recognize him (there is no other word to use, other than "recognize")? Well, if this fact happened, then recognizing that man, recognizing who that man was—not who he was in depth and detail, but recognizing that this man was someone exceptional, uncommon, and irreducible to any kind of analysis—should have been easy. If God became man and came among us, if he came now, if he snuck into our crowd and were here among us, recognizing him (*a priori*, I mean) should be easy: it should be easy to recognize him in his divine value. Why is it easy to recognize him? Because of an exceptionality, an unparalleled exceptionality. I have before me an exceptionality, a man who is exceptional, beyond compare. What does exceptional mean? Why does the exceptional strike you? Why do you feel that something exceptional is "exceptional"? Because it corresponds to the expectations of your heart, however confused and nebulous they might be. It corresponds unexpectedly—unexpectedly!—to the needs of your mind and heart, to the irresistible, undeniable demands of your heart like you could never have imagined or predicted, because there is no one like that man. The exceptional, that is, is, paradoxically, the appearance of what is most natural to us. What is natural for me? That what I desire should happen. Nothing is more natural than this! That what I desire most should happen: this is natural. To come up against something that is absolutely and profoundly natural, because it corresponds to the needs of the heart that nature has given us, is something absolutely exceptional. It is like a strange contradiction: what happens is never exceptional, never truly exceptional, because it fails to adequately respond to the needs of the heart. We attribute exceptionality to something that makes our heart pound because of a correspondence that seems to hold definite value, a correspondence that the next day our heart will disavow and the next year it will undo.

It is the exceptionality with which the figure of Christ appears that makes it easy to recognize him. We must imagine and immerse ourselves in these events, as I said before. We must make ourselves one with them. If we claim to judge these events, if we want to judge them—I don't mean understand them, but judge them substantially, as true or false—we must identify with them sincerely, so that the experience becomes true for us, and our hearts do not doubt the truth. It is easy to recognize it as a divine ontology because it is exceptional: it corresponds to the heart, and one would stay there and would never want to leave—which is the sign of a correspondence with the heart. One would never leave, and would follow him all one's life. And in fact they followed him the remaining three years that he lived.

But imagine those two listening to him for a few hours and then having to go home afterward. He bids them farewell and they go their way silently, silent because they are overcome by the impression of having felt the mystery, of having had a sentiment or presentiment of the mystery. And then they part ways. Each of them goes to his own home. They don't say goodbye to each other, not because they don't say goodbye but because they bid each other farewell without saying goodbye, because they are full of the same thing. The two of them are one and the same, so full are they of the same thing. And Andrew goes into his house and puts down his cloak, and his wife says, "Andrew, what's the matter with you? You're different, what happened to you?" Imagine him bursting into tears as he embraces her, and her being shocked by this and continuing to ask him, "What's wrong with you?" And him holding his wife, who had never felt herself held that way before: he was another person. He was another person! It was him, but it was another. If someone had asked him, "Who are you?" he would have said, "I understand that I have become someone else . . . after hearing that person, that man, I have become another person." My friends, in no uncertain terms, this happened.

Not only is it easy to recognize him, not only was it easy to recognize him in his exceptionality—because "if I don't believe this man, I don't even believe my own eyes anymore"—but it was also easy to understand what kind of morality, that is, what type of relationship came from him; because morality is relating to reality as something created by the Mystery that made it. It is the rightly ordered relationship with reality. It was easy, it was easy for them to understand how easy it was to have a relationship with him, to follow him, to be consistent with what he was, to be consistent with his presence.

There is another page by Saint John that says these things in a spectacular way. It is in the last chapter of his Gospel, the twenty-first. That morning, the boat was coming to the shore and they had not caught any fish. A few hundred meters from the bank they realized that a man was standing there—he had lit a little fire, they could see it from a hundred meters away. The man started conversing with them in a certain way that I will not describe now. John was the first to say, "It is the Lord!" and Saint Peter suddenly threw himself into the lake, and in four strokes reached the shore, and it was the Lord. Meanwhile the others arrived, and no one spoke. They all gathered around in a circle, and no one spoke, they all kept quiet because they all knew that it was the risen Lord: he had already died, and had already shown himself to them after he had risen. He had prepared some roasted fish for them. Everyone sat down and ate. In the almost total silence that hung over on the beach, Jesus, lying down, looked over at his neighbor, who was Simon Peter; he stared at him, and Peter felt the weight of that gaze. Let's imagine how he felt its weight, because he remembered the betrayal of a few weeks prior, and all that he had done—he had even gotten himself called Satan by Christ: "Get behind me, Satan, you are a stumbling block for me, for the destiny of my life" (Matthew 16:23). He remembered all his faults, because when you make a serious mistake, all the other things you have done also come to mind, even those that are less serious. Peter felt as if he were crushed by the weight of his inability, his inability to be a man. And that man next to him opened his mouth and said, "Simon [imagine how Simon must have been trembling], do you love me?" If you try to imagine yourselves in this situation, you will tremble now thinking about it, just thinking about it, thinking about this scene that is so dramatic; dramatic, which is to say, so descriptive of what is human, exposing what is human, exalting what is human, because drama is what exalts the factors that make up the human person—only tragedy annihilates them. Nihilism leads to tragedy, while the encounter with Christ brings drama into your life, because drama is the lived relationship between an "I" and a "thou." Then, like a breath, like a breath, Peter answered. His response was barely audible, like a breath. He didn't dare, but ... "I don't know how, yes, Lord, I love you; I don't know how, but I do." "Yes, Lord. I don't know how, I can't tell you how, but...."

In short, it was very easy to retain—to live—the relationship with that man. One simply had to adhere to the sympathy that he brought forth, a profound sympathy, like that dizzying and visceral sympathy between a child and his mother, which is sympathy in the intense meaning of the word. It was enough to adhere to the sympathy that he aroused. Because, after everything that Peter had done to him, and the betrayal, he heard him say, "Simon, do you love me?" Three times. And the third time he suspected, perhaps, that there was some doubt within Jesus's question, and he answered more fully, "Lord, you know everything, you know that I love you. My human sympathy is for you; my human sympathy is for you, Jesus of Nazareth."

Learning from an extraordinary presence happens through a profound correspondence of feeling: this is the logic of knowledge and the logic of morality which living with that individual made necessary—only this. To learn is an ultimate sympathy. As it is with a child and his mother: he can make mistakes a thousand times a day, a hundred thousand times a day, but woe to you if you try to take him away from his mother! If he could understand the question, "Do you love this woman?" and answer it, imagine what a "yes" he would cry out. The more the mistakes he had made, the more he would cry out "yes" to affirm it. (I'm speaking as a man to men and women, who, being young, have fewer preconceptions; or rather they are chock-full of preconceptions, but those of the grown-ups.)

In the end, then, what does the morality of sympathy toward him demand that you do, that you carry out? That you observe him, or that active observation that is called "following." That you follow him. And indeed, they went back with him the next day, and he went back with them the third day, because he lived in a neighboring village. He began to go fishing with them, and in the afternoons he would visit them on the shore while they were mending their nets. And when, now and then, he began to go to the inland villages, he would stop by and say, "Will you come with me?" Some would go and some would not, but eventually they all ended up going. They ended up going for a few hours, then more hours, then the whole day, then he started staying out at night, and they followed him, forgetting their homes. . . . They did not forget their homes! There was something greater than their homes, something from which their homes were born, from which their love for their wives was born, something that could save the love with which they looked at their children and watched with concern as they grew up. There was something that saved all of this more than their feeble strength and exceedingly weak imagination could. What could they do, in the face of nasty years of famine or the dangers their children were facing? They followed him! Every day they listened to what he said: all the people were there, gaping, and they were there gaping even more. One never tired of hearing him speak.

And then, he was good. "He took a child, embraced him, and said, 'Woe to him who harms a single hair on the least of these children!'" (Matthew 18:2-6, Mark 9:36-42). And he was not talking about hurting the child physically, which, up to a certain point, people have more restraint about (although this is no longer true, and it is not the only sad sign of the times). No, he was talking about causing the child scandal, which hurts him, even if no one thinks so. He was good. When he saw that funeral, he immediately inquired, "Who is it?" "It's a teenager, whose father died recently." And the boy's mother wailed and wailed behind the coffin, not according to the custom of that time, but according to the nature of a mother's heart, which expresses itself freely. He took a step toward her and said, "Woman, do not weep!" (Luke 7:11-13). Is there anything more unjust than saying to a woman whose child has died, who has been left alone, "Woman, do not weep"? And yet it was instead a sign of compassion, affection, a participation in her endless pain. He said to the son, "Get up!" And he gave her back her son. But he could not give her back her son without saying anything; otherwise, he would have retained the distant gravitas of a prophet and wonder-worker, a man of miracles. "Woman, do not weep," he said. And he gave her back her son. But first he said, "Woman, do not weep."

Imagine perceiving him like this every day for a year, or for two—sensing that he was so good, sensing that he had such power over nature that it seemed to be at his service. That evening he went out in the boat with them and it was night. At a certain point, a raging wind arose, a terrible storm was suddenly unleashed on the Sea of Galilee, and they were about to sink. The boat was full of water. He was asleep; he was so tired that he didn't even notice the storm and was sleeping in the stern. One of them said, "Master, wake up, wake up, we are sinking!" And he raised his head, stretched out his hand, and "commanded the wind and the sea, and immediately there was a great calm." Those men, the Gospel concludes, those men, afraid, said among themselves, "Who is this man?" (Matthew 8:23-27; Luke 8:22-25)

This question introduces the problem of Christ in the history of the world, until the end of the world. The problem of Christ: this very question, precisely this one, which is found in the eighth chapter of the Gospel of Saint Luke. These were people who knew him very well, who knew his family, they knew him like the back of their hands, they followed him, they had left their homes! But so disproportionate was that man's way of acting, so inconceivable, so masterful, that it came naturally to his friends to say, "Who is this man?" That is to say, "What is behind this?" There is nothing the human person desires more than this "incomprehensibility." There is nothing the person desires more ardently, albeit fearfully, without realizing it, than this inexplicable presence. For this is God. This is the sign and the connection with the Mystery. In fact, it is the same question that his enemies asked him at the end, before they killed him. A few weeks before they killed him, as they argued with him, they said to him, "How long will you keep us in suspense? Tell us where you are from and who you are" (John 10:24). They had the registry, and he was one they had enrolled in the registry thirty-three years earlier. Of no man on earth can we say, "Who is this who does such things?", compelled by astonishment and by the disproportion between what we imagine to be possible and the reality before us. Like the time he fed more than five thousand men, not counting women and children—he fed them mysteriously—then disappeared, because they wanted to make him king. They said, out of economic interests: "This is truly the Messiah who is to come into the world!", immediately reverting to the common mentality by which they had always lived, that everyone had—as indeed their leaders taught, the Messiah was to be a mighty man who would have given Israel, their people, supremacy over the world (John 6:14-15). He eluded them, and many of them guessed that he had gone to Capernaum. So they went around the lake to go and retrieve him, in the early evening on the Sabbath. They went to the synagogue, because it was the place they would most likely find him. In fact, when he spoke, he always took his cue from the biblical passage that was proposed to the people for that day, from the scroll that the attendant chose. And, sure enough, there he was in the synagogue, saying that their fathers had eaten manna but that he would feed them with something much greater, his own word: his word was truth. He gave them truth to eat, truth to drink, the truth about life and about the world. The door opens in the back, and in comes the group who had been looking for him, who had been after him, let's say. They were looking for him. They were seeking him for the wrong reason, because they wanted to make him king—not because they were struck by the sign that he was, by the mystery of his person, which the power of his deeds assured, but because they had an interest. They sought him for a material interest. The motive was wrong, but they sought him. They were seeking him. He was born so that the whole world might seek him. He was moved, and suddenly—for, as a man like us, ideas came to him through circumstances—a fantastic idea occurred to him. He shifted the meaning of what he was saying and exclaimed, "Not my word, but my body will I give you to eat, my blood to drink!" (John 6:48-54). The cue—finally the politicians and the journalists and the broadcasters of that time had their cue—"He is mad! Who can give people his own flesh to eat?" When he said something that was pressing to him, but people did not understand and were scandalized by what he said, he would not explain it but would repeat it instead. He repeated, "Truly, I tell you, whoever does not eat my flesh cannot enter into the understanding of reality, cannot enter into the realm of being to understand reality, cannot enter the depths of reality, for this is the truth." They all left, saying, "He is mad, he is mad." *Durus est hic sermo*, "He has a strange way of speaking" (John 6:60). Until, in the twilight of the evening, he was left with the usual twelve. They too kept silent, with their heads down. Imagine the scene in the not-so-large synagogue of Capernaum—it was like one of our schoolrooms with thirty or forty seats. "Do you also want to leave? I will not take back what I have said: do you, too, wish to go away?" And Simon Peter, stubborn Peter, said, "Master, we do not understand what you say either, but if we leave you, where shall we go? You alone have words that give meaning to life" (John 6:67-68). Kafka: "There is a goal, but no way." That man was the way. "If we go away from you, where shall we go? What will be the road, what could be the road? You are the road."

***

Those two, John and Andrew, and those twelve, Simon and the rest, told their wives, and some of those wives went with them. At a certain point many went with them and followed him: they left their homes and went with them. And they also told other friends, who did not necessarily leave their homes, yet participated in their sympathy, participated in their positive attitude of awe and faith in that man. And these friends told other friends, and these in turn other friends, and then others again. Thus the first century passed, and these friends invaded the second century with their faith, and meanwhile they invaded the geographical world as well. They reached Spain at the end of the first century and as far as India in the second century. And then those in the second century told it to others who lived after them, and these told others after them, like a great stream that swelled, like a great river that swelled, and eventually they told my mother—my mother. And my mother told me when I was little, and I too say, "Master, neither do I understand what you say, but if we leave you, where shall we go? You alone have words that correspond to the heart." Which is the law of reason: the law of reason is the comparison with the heart. I was told about a friend of ours who is not Catholic, who, reading one of our texts, remarked, "Here I find the word 'heart' used not as I mean it, because I understand the heart to be the reference point of feelings—I have one feeling, he has another. Whereas here it is not used that way; it is the same for everyone, this heart spoken of in *The Religious Sense* is the same for everyone, it is the same for me and for you."[48] If the heart is the seat of the need for truth, for

Recognizing Christ

beauty, for goodness, for justice, the seat of the thirst for happiness, who among us can evade these needs, who? They constitute our nature, mine and yours, and that is why we are more united than "absent" and estranged from one another, as we normally are. And the last Korean man, the last man from Vladivostok, the last man from the farthest and most remote region of the earth is united to me precisely because of this.

From that evening, a flow of humanity was born that has reached up to *now*, to *me*. As my mother belonged to this flow, so do I belong to it, and by telling many friends about it I make them part of this stream as well.

Even if you already know it, it's worth rereading (because it's not a waste of time) the letter I received, and unfortunately discovered too late, from a young man suffering from AIDS who died two days after writing to me.

> Dear Fr. Giussani, I write to you calling you "dear" even though I do not know you, I have never seen you nor heard you speak. But to tell you the truth, I can say that I do know you in that—if I have understood anything of *The Religious Sense* and of what Ziba tells me—I know you by faith and, I now add, thanks to the faith. I am just writing to say thank you. Thank you for having given a meaning to this arid life of mine: I am a high school classmate of Ziba's, with whom I have always maintained a friendly relationship since, though I did not share his position, I was always struck by his humanity, his selfless availability [which is the only way we can cry out to another and to the whole world, "Christ is true."] Of this troubled life I think I have reached the end of the line, carried by that train called AIDS that leaves no respite for anyone. Now saying this does not make me afraid anymore. Ziba always used to tell me that the important thing in life is to have a true interest and to follow it. I pursued this interest many times, but it was never the true one. Now I have seen the true one, I see him, I have met him, and I am beginning to know him, to call him by name: his name is Christ. I don't even know what that means or how I can say these things, but when I see

the face of my friend or read *The Religious Sense* that is keeping me company, and I think of you or the things Ziba tells me about you, everything seems clearer—everything, even my evil and my pain. My life, which had been flattened and made barren, made like a smooth stone where everything runs off like water, receives a jolt of meaning and significance that sweeps away the wicked thoughts and sorrows. Or rather, it embraces them and makes them true, rendering my grubby and putrid body a sign of his presence. Thank you, Don Giussani, because you have communicated this faith—or, as you call it, this Event—to me. Now I feel at peace, free and at peace. When Ziba used to recite the Angelus in front of me who blasphemed to his face, I hated him and told him he was a coward because the only thing he knew how to do was to say those stupid prayers in front of me. Now, when I stutteringly try to say it with him, I realize that the coward was me because I couldn't even see an inch from my nose the truth that was in front of me. Thank you, Don Giussani, is the only thing that a man like me can say to you. Thank you because in my tears I can say that dying like this now has a meaning. Not because it is more beautiful—I have a great fear of dying—but because now I know that there is someone who loves me and that I too can perhaps be saved and that I too can pray that my fellow patients might encounter and see as I have seen and encountered. So I feel useful—just think, only by using my voice I feel useful, with the only thing that I can still use well I can be useful. I who have thrown away my life can do good by simply saying the Angelus. It is striking, but even if it were an illusion this is too human and too reasonable, as you say in *The Religious Sense*, not to be true. Ziba attached to my bed the phrase of Saint Thomas: "Man's life consists in the affection which principally sustains him and in which he finds his greatest satisfaction."[49] I think my greatest satisfaction is to have known you [I've never seen him!] by writing this letter to you, but the still greater one is that in God's mercy, if he wills it, I will know you there where everything will be new, good, and true. New, good, and true like the friendship that you have brought into the lives of many people and of which I can say, "I was there, too." I too in this wretched life have seen and participated in this new, good, and true event. Pray for me, I will continue to feel useful for the time I have left by praying for you and for the movement. I embrace you. Andrea.[50]

Two thousand years are burned away by this letter. He was not yesterday, he is today. He is not today for me, but today *for you*, no matter what position you take: change it, if it needs to be changed! Every morning, I too understand that I must change it, because I am responsible for many things he has given me. All I am saying is that this event or presence belongs to today—today! That human flow that we talked about, I bring it into your life today. There is only God, God alone, yesterday, today, and forever. A great event, as Kierkegaard said, can only be present, because the past, a dead person, cannot change us. If something changes us, then it is present: "he is, if he changes," states one of our texts.[51]

But there is more than just this most beautiful letter. You will have read (either in the newspapers or in *Traces*[52]) the prayer written by our friends in Turin who lost all their family members in the recent tragedy in Piedmont.[53] "In this terrible and great hour we want to thank the Lord, our God and Father, for having given us, in Christ, Francesco, Cecilia, Lucia, and Cecilia. Through them, you, O Christ, began to make yourself known to us with baptism, education, Lucia's belonging to the movement, and the birth of Cecilia—which we welcomed as a miracle. Grant, O Christ, that now that they are in you while you make all of reality, they might help us recognize you more and more in every instant of life."[54] After two thousand years he is now: for Alberto and Mario, he is now. Cry out to him, who is now, that he may bear your coldness, your ignorance, your distance! When I was a boy and got sick and was in bed with a fever, I saw people as being far, far away; I saw the room and walls as being far, far away; I saw the furniture as being very distant and I was afraid to find myself alone in a vast, terribly long space. And when my mother entered the room, I saw her as tiny, almost nonexistent. It is a sickness that makes us see him as far away, because he is God, the present. He "is" because he is present. Whatever is not in our present experience, or in no way could be found in our present experience, whatever would not be in any way in our present experience does not exist—it would not exist.

There is a third testimony I want to mention. Seven friends of ours, four women of the *Memores Domini* and three priests, two of them from Rome, from the seminary of Monsignor Massimo Camisasca[55]—all from the movement—are in the vast Siberia, in Novosibirsk. It is the largest diocese, the largest parish in the world, stretching five thousand kilometers from Novosibirsk to Vladivostok. And they travel this whole area, four hundred kilometers every week. They recently held the first Catholic synod in Siberia, in the city of Vladivostok, which is near Japan at the eastern end of Siberia. And the bishops invited our people too. They have been there for three years and have a small group of friends who have asked to be baptized; some of them are living the life of CL. One of them recounted what happened in his life. He is a young boy of seventeen years.

> I met the movement right after my encounter with the Catholic Church. At that time, I knew practically nothing about the Christian life, and I understood even less. I came across a group of relatively young people, most of whom were students, and some Italians who spoke little or no Russian. I heard them talk about life, about work; they spoke about their Christian experience, about their first encounter with Christ; they also sang together and had fun. Then they went to Mass together and would sometimes recite Vespers. I had the impression that they were good friends, yet, truly, there was something strange about it to me: why had these strangers come from so far away, why? Why did they come all the way here where it is so cold, and life is not as comfortable as it is back where they came from? And then people who were so young, different from one another and yet good friends, why were they together? It is probably precisely in this,

and even in this, that the grace of the first encounter lies: when you intuitively sense exactly what you need in life, you feel something that corresponds to your heart, something good that reawakens curiosity and desire in you, so that each time you relive the first encounter without fully recognizing why. And in fact only later did I begin to intuit and to understand that in this companionship there is someone present, before whom everyone bows and who brings together people who at first glance could never be together. I think that this was a kind of 'extraordinary moment' for me, when I recognized the presence of Christ, when I discovered him in that companionship. I realized that I am loved [like Andrea], loved very much by Jesus, precisely through these people whom he himself has placed beside me and who accompany me. I have been in the movement of CL for three years already and this helps me. I can say that now I experience a zest for life and this seems to me to be very important [it is the opposite of what dominates today: the loss of the zest for life is a symptom of what is macabre in the current culture]. In fact, there are many different aspects of life: work, rest, study, and vacation, and seeing the meaning in every aspect of life, recognizing that God became an event in our lives—Christianity is precisely this. Nothing happens randomly, nothing just happens, and every moment of history can testify to the presence of Christ here and now. I have many friends, I meet a lot of people and I always feel a great sorrow that they have not yet experienced the grace of the first encounter that would enable them to grasp his presence and compel them to follow him. I would like to share with everyone I meet the desire to experience the taste for life ['taste': taste is such a natural term, so carnal and so divine: it is a foretaste of eternal happiness, that eternal taste which is the aim of being alive]. Of course, my experience is still small, but I ask that in all aspects of life I may bear witness to Christ, present here and now. Josif.[56]

And indeed, as it is for Josif, the greatest surprise for me as a Christian is to experience now, to discover now, the correspondence with the heart that he is. When a journalist approached one of Mother Teresa of Calcutta's sisters in India—a very young sister, not yet twenty years old—and asked her a few questions, among other things she said, "I remember picking a man up off the street and bringing him into our house." "And what did that man say?" "He did not grumble, he did not swear, he only said, 'I have lived on the street like an animal and I'm about to die like an angel, loved and cared for. Sister, I am about to return to the house of God,' and then died. I have never seen a smile like the one on the face of that man."[57] The journalist replied, "Why is it that even the greatest sacrifices seem to demand no effort from you, that you experience no fatigue?" Then Mother Teresa interjected, "Jesus is the one to whom we do everything. We love and acknowledge Jesus, today."[58] Today: yesterday is gone. What was there yesterday is either here today, or it is no more.

I'm sorry I cannot read it all, because it is too long, but I would like to quote at least an excerpt of a letter from our friend Gloria, the young teacher who went to Kampala in Africa to work with Rose Busingye.[59] She writes: "Nothing here is immediate for me [nothing is comfortable for me, nothing is easy for me]. And in some moments, I felt a kind of inability to stay in front of people who were sick, dirty, without the slightest sanitation. [Who could make her do this? The memory of something two thousand years ago? No! Something now. A presence that is now.] One morning, as I was greeting Rose, she told me, 'Pray to Our Lady that today you might not be frightened by seeing how Christ presents himself to you.' With these words in my heart, I went with Claudia to the juvenile prison. Everything disgusted me: the stench, the filth, the scabies, the lice. And at that moment I understood that my entreaty coincided with the position of my person." Bent over the sick person, or over the child prisoner, bent over in that position: her entreaty, the entreaty for being, which is what the human heart asks for (because even if one doesn't think about it, the heart cries out for being), the entreaty for being, the entreaty for happiness, the entreaty for truth, the entreaty for goodness, justice, beauty—this entreaty coincided with the very position that she assumed.

But the most significant news in these days, perhaps the most significant of all our history, is what happened in Brasília. Please go and read the story in *Traces* about the killing of Edimàr, a young boy who was among the worst delinquent boys in all Brasília—a murderer more than once, because his gang is a band of assassins. At the beginning of the year, a teacher in the *Memores Domini*, originally from Lebanon but living in Brazil, went to his class. She speaks our language. Edimàr was shocked; he too wanted to have eyes full of blue like hers and not dark, black, and dirty eyes like his own. He vowed to change. The gang leader understood that there was something wrong and immediately put him to the test, ordering him to go kill someone. Edimàr said, "I won't kill anyone anymore." And the leader replied, "I will kill you, then," and killed him. He is the second martyr of our history.[60]

***

What is the formula that summarizes the whole figure of Christ in itself, the figure of Christ as a man, who was registered by the administration at Bethlehem, and is present now to rouse and demand the lives and hearts of each of us, so that through us the whole world might recognize him and be happier, so that everyone in the world might be happier, might know "why," might die like Andrea? The concise formula that describes the whole dynamic of Jesus is that he was sent by the Father.

Why did Jesus, who was God, the Word of God, the expression of God and therefore the origin of the world, become man? Why did he enter the womb of a fifteen-year-old girl? Why was he begotten in that womb, born as a child, why did he grow up into a youth, an adolescent, a man, a man in his thirties? Why did he speak the way we have heard him speak, and strike Andrea, and strike our friends at Villa Turro (the AIDS patients our friends care for), and strike Edimàr?[61] Why did he become a man and act in history like this, become present in history like this? To carry out the plan of another. Jesus himself uses the ultimate word to point to the origin of everything, that from which, therefore, life itself is born: the Father. His life is defined as a call from the Father to carry out a mission: life is vocation.

This is the Christian definition of life: life is vocation. And vocation is to fulfill a mission, to perform a task, which God determines for each person through the mundane, everyday circumstances, moment by moment, that he allows us to pass through. This is why Christ is the ideal of our life, insofar as life is an attempt to respond, a desire to respond to God's call: vocation, God's call, the plan that the Mystery has for me. Because in this moment, if I am sincere, if I am thoughtful, I understand that I do not make myself. There is nothing so evident—not even you who are two meters from me—nothing so obvious as the fact that in this instant I do not give myself being, I do not give myself hair, I do not give myself eyes, I do not give myself a nose, I do not give myself teeth, I do not give myself my heart, I do not give myself my soul, I do not give myself thoughts and feelings. Everything is given: that I might fulfill his plan, a plan that is not mine, through all things, through writing, through speaking, through the Angelus (as Andrea said), through everything, everything. "Whether you eat or drink," says Saint Paul, making the most banal comparison one could think of, "whether you stay awake or sleep," "whether you live or die"—he says in another passage—everything is the glory of Christ, that is, the plan of God (1 Corinthians 10:31; 1 Thessalonians 5:10; Romans 14:8).

Christ is the ideal of life. He whom John and Andrew heard speaking was the ideal of life. This is why their hearts leapt, why they went home in silence, why Andrew embraced his wife that evening as he had never done before, without being able to say anything. They had encountered the ideal of life. They could not express it this way right away, poor men. They said it a few years later. After that day they went all over the world to say it: Christ is the ideal of life.

Recognizing Christ

What does it mean that Christ is the ideal of life? It means that he is the ideal for the way we treat all of nature; he is the ideal for the way we live affection, and therefore the ideal by which we understand, look at, feel, treat, and live the relationship with our woman or our man, with our parents and our children. He is the ideal according to which we approach others and live our relationship with them, that is, with society as a whole and as a companionship of men and women. What is the characteristic that this ideal instills in our way of treating one another, in our way of treating everything, from nature—by which I mean everything that exists, because I can treat poorly or unjustly even this microphone here, as I did before without realizing it—down to our mother and father? The characteristic lies in two words that have the same root, but one is the beginning and the other is the end of the trajectory of every action. The first is called gratitude. Why? Because of what I said earlier: that nothing is more evident at this moment, to me and to you, than the fact that you don't make yourself, that everything is given. There is another in you who is more you than you are yourself, you spring from a source that is not you: this source is the mystery of being. Thus, analogously, you understand that all things are made by another. You, as a person, are the consciousness of nature: the "I" is the level at which nature becomes aware of itself.[62] Just as I become aware that I do not make myself, so I become aware that none of nature makes itself, it is given—given, a gift. Therefore, I am grateful: gratitude as the foundation and premise of every action, every attitude.

What does this gratitude instill in all actions? It instills an aspect, a nuance, an aura of gratuitousness, pure gratuitousness, that gratuitousness of which Ada Negri spoke—as we have recalled so many times—in one of her unparallelled poems, which expresses this in the best way I can imagine: "You love, and think not to be loved: for every / flower that blossoms or fruit that blushes / or child that is born, to the God of the fields / and the generations you give thanks in your heart."[63] You love, you like the flower, not because you smell it, but because it is there; you look at the ripening fruit not because you bite it, but because it is there. You look at the child not because he is yours, but because he is there. This is absolute purity. Please, make an effort to immerse yourselves in this absoluteness of purity. A tinge of this purity, of this gratuity enters into us even without our being aware of it; it almost naturally enters into our every action. So that if any attitude of mine toward you does not contain this gratuitousness, a hint of this gratuitousness, it is ugly, is a fallen relationship, fallen and prone to falling. It is a relationship on the cusp of collapse, of its undoing. Only this purity of gratuitousness keeps things from unraveling, prevents anything from being undone, maintains all things that were in the past, that were born in the past, and keeps them in the present; so that my person in the present moment is enriched by all that it did yesterday and the day before, and nothing is useless, as our friend Andrea said two days before dying.

Because of this, the outcome of following Jesus as the ideal of life, of life as vocation, the outcome—as the Gospel says—is the hundredfold (Mark 10:29-30). Things become more powerful, my relationship with you becomes more powerful; it's as if we were born together. I didn't know you until a few years ago, and I have no particular interest (in the sense of a gain or profit), none. We are not together for profit. And I may get along with you very well, regardless of what you think, but this is not why I am a friend to you. Thus there is a more powerful richness in all relationships, in the way of looking at a flower, in the way of looking at stars, in the way of looking at plants and leaves, in the way of bearing with myself—as I impudently demand that you stay here another five minutes—in the way I think about the sins I committed yesterday, or the day before: "Lord forgive me, grant me, a sinner, your forgiveness," but saying this does not disappoint me nor depress me, it makes me truer, and if I did not say it I would be less true, because I am one, a sinner.

From this richness comes a capacity for fruitfulness that no one else has, fruitfulness that is the communication of your own nature, your own richness, your own intelligence, your own will, your own heart, your own time, your own life. And to say, "I would lay down my life for each of you," every one of us would say it for every one of the rest. Every one of us does say it. If one does not say it, it is because he has never thought about it, and if he has never thought about it, it is because he has never thought of it while becoming aware of the presence of Christ. If instead he starts from this presence, he says, "I would lay down my life—but Jesus, help me, okay?" It is fruitfulness in work, a passion for work that is not for gain or for personal taste or for its bearing on my standing in society; it is a love for work as a perfection of action, whatever the outcome. It is fruitfulness that is love for giving what I am, for giving you myself, that is, for giving oneself to one's children. It is love for all that enters and will enter into relationship with one's children, love for others who are also sons and daughters, who are also one's children, love for everyone: for the people. A fruitfulness at work, a fruitfulness before one's children, a fruitfulness in the life of the people. In short, the ideal of life becomes the good of others, good for others: good for others, your good, my good. This is the end for which God made the world: the good of all, the good. It is the opposite of Bobbio's essay on evil, which is serious and moving—I believe it is moving from the few pages I have read—but the plan of a father is the good of the son.[64] The ideal of life becomes the good.

**

Now I ask you to please pay attention in these last five minutes, because what I am about to say is the most incisive of all we have said so far; it is the most pointed consequence of today's theme. There is a form of vocation in which one chooses an unexpected and unfathomable path, a path unthought of and unthinkable in anyone's mind, and it is called—excuse me for saying it right away—*virginity*. It is a form of vocation that pierces through, as light pierces glass (the word "pierce" is rather indispensable), a form of vocation that pierces through the most natural needs as they present themselves in everybody's experience. Those who take this road have the natural urges that everyone else has: this form of vocation pierces through the most natural needs as they present themselves to experience by paradoxically realizing them according to a new potentiality.

In them, with this life, with this form of vocation, work becomes obedience. Because everyone goes to work for various motives, in which there is also that note we call gratuitousness: but it is in virginity that work becomes all gratuity, it tends to become completely gratuitous. Why do you go to your law firm, why do you go to the class you teach? Payday, or career, or the sheer fact that one must work—truly, these fade with the passage of time. Only the will for the good of others remains: that the will of God be done. In other words, work becomes obedience. What is obedience? Obedience is performing an action to affirm another. What is action? Action is the phenomenon by which the "I" affirms itself, realizes itself. To realize myself, the action that I take I do not take for myself, but for another: this is obedience. The law of action is another, it is affirming another, it is love for the Word, it is love for Christ. Work is love for Christ.

If work becomes obedience, love for a man or a woman is exalted. A man who exalts himself in the physical sense of the term is a man who stands up straight, in the full height of his person. Love for woman is exalted as a sign of the perfection, the attraction for which man is made. This is what Leopardi sensed.[65] At a certain point in his life, from which he later lapsed, he sensed that the face of woman was a sign: he had loved many women, but in that moment he intuited that it was not this face or that one, but another face, with a capital "F," it was a woman with a capital "W"—to whom he wrote that beautiful hymn—that he sought. Love for a woman is exalted as a sign of the perfection and attractiveness of the beautiful, the good, the true and the just, which is Christ, because the perfection, the source of attraction, the source of the beautiful, the good, the true, and the just is the Word of God. What shines forth, as Leopardi said in the hymn *To His Lady*, in a landscape, or in the beauty of a dream, or in the beauty of a face, is the divine that lies at the origin of everything; in the face of the other—the other *par excellence* which is woman for man, and vice versa—it shines forth, shines forth in an ineffable way, which one cannot put into words.[66] The one who managed best to say it, in my opinion, was Leopardi, who did not say it outright but was on the verge of saying it. Allow me, so that these things do not seem abstract to you, to read a letter that a friend of ours was sent by her ex-boyfriend. They had been together for three years. After three years, she sensed that her vocation was to virginity and she told him that she was going to take some time to verify it.

The ex-boyfriend writes to her, saying, "Dearest, I want to enclose only a few words, since everything is already sealed in our hearts forever [forever! Nothing is eliminated]. I am moved, that is, moved to awe at what is being accomplished in your life, or, to put it better, at he who is accomplishing it. It is a joy that will lead me in time to the destiny of good that has taken you with himself. Even the pain that assails me, at some times stronger than at others, for what I did to you at certain moments of our acquaintance, is suffused with a mercy that makes it truer. It remains a mystery, but one that is already revealing itself. The whole fullness of the relationship between us, of that piece of history that we walked together, is better explained this way. I like to believe that every instant you spent with me, even in the face of my incapacity, is not lost [forever!] and has served, that is, has been used by Christ to accompany you to him. I ask your forgiveness, that is, to grant me your posture of the beggar, in the certainty that you have given me a greater love by belonging to the *Memores Domini*, that is, that you have loved me more by doing this than by marrying me. I thank you for this expectation of yours and I pray to Our Lady that you will always have faces full of hope around you, as there are now, to protect you and love you in every step you take. I have given you an icon of Christ, a sign of his Incarnation [a concept that Eastern Orthodoxy has understood very well] so that you will always be comforted by his presence and so that you will remember to pray for me, for the task entrusted to me now of loving Elisabetta, for my relatives and our friends, but above all so that you will never abandon that embrace of the Holy Spirit that is the movement and his mysterious sentinel."

He has understood. Do you understand that he understood? Work becomes obedience, love for a woman becomes the supreme sign of the perfection of the attractiveness she exerts on us, of the happiness that awaits us. And a people, instead of being the subject of a human history full of quarrels and struggles, becomes the subject of a history of men and women, of a stream, of a river of consciences that are gradually enlightened by yielding, if only in death, to the glory of Christ.

It is called charity; these changes are called charity. Work that becomes obedience is called charity. Love for a woman that becomes a sign of ultimate perfection, ultimate beauty, is called charity. And a people who becomes the history of Christ, the reign of Christ, the glory of Christ, is charity. Because charity is looking at a presence, any presence, with our souls gripped by passion for Christ, by tenderness for Christ. There are experiences of gladness and joy that are only possible under these conditions. Otherwise gladness and joy are two words we must rip out of our vocabulary, because there is no possibility of gladness and joy on other terms. There may be contentment, satisfaction, whatever you like, but gladness does not exist, for gladness demands absolute gratuitousness, which is possible only with the presence of the divine, with the anticipation of happiness, and joy is its momentary explosion, when God wills it, to sustain the heart of a person or of a people in significant moments of their education. However, excuse me, that work may become obedience, that love for a woman may become a sign, as Leopardi intuited, that the people may not be a tangle of faces but the advancement of the kingdom of God—this charity is the law for everyone, not for virgins alone. It is the law for everyone, yes, it is the law for all. Virginity is the visible form of life that recalls everyone to the same ideal—for everyone—which is Christ, for whom alone it is worth it to live and to die, to work, to love a woman, to bring up children, to sustain and help a people. This charity is for all, but some are called to the sacrifice of virginity precisely so that they may be present among everyone to recall this ideal that is for all. You should have read, in *Why the Church?*, if you have gotten that far, the concept of miracle.[67] A miracle is an event—as it is defined there—that inexorably points back to God, a phenomenon that necessarily makes you think of God. The miracle of miracles, more than all the miracles of Lourdes, more than all the miracles of any shrine in the world, the miracle of miracles, that is to say, the phenomenon that inexorably compels you to think of Jesus, is a beautiful twenty-year-old girl who embraces virginity.

The Church is the place of this road and of all the working, fruitful, flourishing influences on those who walk together in the company that God creates, in which all roads come together. The Church is the place where all these people are enriched, where they give themselves and are enriched by the gift of others. The Church is truly a moving place—of humanity that is moved; it is the place of humanity, where humanity grows and increases, continually expelling anything spurious that enters into it, because we are human; but the Church is human, so men and women are human when they expel what is spurious and love what is pure. The Church is something truly moving.

The fight with nihilism, against nihilism, is living this "being moved."

3

God and Man

"SEE, I AM ESTABLISHING a new way in the world. Do you not perceive it? It has already begun" (Isaiah 43:19). All too often we don't even see it ourselves, when in fact we are its immediate craftsmen, its decisive protagonists. He makes use of this shovel that I am—mangled by time, neglected, reluctant to be taken into his hands, by those two hands of his. To be taken into those two hands is the only warmth in life, the only secure warmth, which makes one want to embrace everyone—with all the distinctions one could possibly imagine, but in the end, everyone all the same.

So you understand how distressed I would be if it weren't for my abandonment to those two hands that hold this shovel that I am; it would be an unbearable pain, it would be a helplessness not to be able to accomplish—or to seem to not be able to accomplish—in each of you what has been said thus far about obedience, an anguish for all of us who brought you the message (the message came through our flesh—my flesh and my teeth, my eyes and my heart—through us, who are responsible before God and Christ for the fact that your lives have been upended by this message, this invitation, this continual urging, this continual reminder.) To be obedient, it is necessary that the one whom you obey has the

God and Man

charity to share in the sacrifices that he calls you to make, to share with you the sacrifices that he calls you to perform. It would lead us to despair, if not to surrender to those hands—to those hands that hold the handle of the spade that I am—that, after having filled you with his words, his memory, his presence, we cannot follow you one by one, sharing every gesture with you, sharing every rush of anticipation and expectation with you, sharing even the weakness of every skeptical and nihilistic thought with you, sharing one step after another with you, as if we were mothers and you were little children.

But we do not think about you or look at you except in this way. And if you understand clearly this martyrdom of ours, you will understand more clearly that without him—him, not me—you can do nothing. Without his Spirit, without the strength of his Spirit, nothing is in you, nothing would remain in you, nothing! And everything would be hostile to you and negative, everything would become negative, like time; there would be nothing in you other than the time of everyone else, the time of everyone whose every moment goes toward death, every instant corrupts, deceives and corrupts, corrupts and deceives.

This is a feeling, a passion that almost crushes our hearts: I believe I am speaking for all the others who are called to share directly with me in the response that all of you must give with us to God; a response not to an abstract God but to Jesus, in this world. I am convinced that you understand this. I am not saying it out of emotion, to communicate an emotion; I am saying it to communicate a reason, the most immediate reason for being like John on the shoulder of Jesus at the Last Supper, as we saw in the painting on the Easter Poster of 1990, or like Simon in the twenty-first chapter of Saint John's Gospel.[68]

"Without me you can do nothing" (John 15:5). So the memory of you is everything, and this memory is begging for you. We must push on the shell that covers every hour of our days: let it crack and let the hour itself be filled with this surrender to you, this certainty of you, this expectation that is mathematically—how ugly!—and lovingly sure, which is a love of yours and a love of mine as a certainty in expectation.

***

Now I will propose an important reflection by which I mean to summarize the content of the previous conversations, and briefly indicate their most striking conclusions.

I prepared this in advance, my friends, because I am always thinking of you. One need not have a child born from one's own womb for this to be true—just as a mother is always thinking about her child. But much more than a child in the womb, we carry the meaning of that child, we carry the reason that it is worthwhile for a mother to carry him in her womb and think about him for years—years upon years!—usually only to be deceived and disenchanted by the passage of time.

But when what we carry in our hearts comes about—the message that was given to us, somehow; the message that welled up in our own hearts, somehow—when we bring into the world what we hold in our hearts, then it is right: it is right for a mother to conceive a child, to tremble for nine months, to tremble when the child is born, to embrace him, whatever he may be like, and to accompany him into life (that is, to educate him) and, from an ever greater distance, accompany him until death.

We cry out this announcement of ours, this reawakening of ours, to the whole world; that is, to the world of the house and the family, the world of our movement, the world of the diocese and the local Church, the world of the universal Church, the world of our poor, wretched homeland, the world of this Europe that is the world's bloodsucker, the world of the "world" that is awakening to rights that replace heaven and God—but when they have gained them, they will only have a ghostly vision of fields of corpses (as T.S. Eliot says in describing the religion of the withered child).[69]

This path of ours, the path of these days, has been planned!

God and Man

a) Do you remember the piece of music we were listening to yesterday morning?

> *Ave, verum Corpus natum*
> *de Maria virgine;*
> *vere passum, immolatum*
> *in cruce pro homine;*
> *cuius latus perforatum*
> *fluxit aqua et sanguine!*
> *Esto nobis praegustatum*
> *mortis in examine.*
>
> Hail, true body born
> of the Virgin Mary!
> Truly afflicted, immolated
> on the cross for humankind;
> from whose pierced side
> blood and water flowed!
> Be a foretaste [of the heavenly banquet] for us
> in the trial of death.

May I have a foretaste of you in life, O Lord, as I will want to perceive you in the moment when you judge me at the end.

God, the Mystery that makes all things, that Mystery of which the three hundred representatives of various religions together with the Cardinal of Milan rightly reminded the whole world in that brief procession of theirs in Milan, Mystery conceived in three hundred different ways, or rather imagined, and then defined with fear and trembling: that Mystery has involved itself with the human person.

The first time I was invited by the Buddhist monks of Mount Koya, in the cultural center of the city of Nagoya (which was packed as never before, the director told me), with what awkwardness did I speak about Christianity! For nine tenths of the lecture, or more, I spoke about the Mystery that reveals itself in the harmony of things, which is their theme, which is why they adore—adore!—every blade of grass, every thorn of a thistle, every hair of the head. They know that there is the Mystery, but they do not know the way to reach it, and they imagine it thus. How awkward when, with only three minutes left, I said to myself, "I must say it, I must say it!" And I said it: "This universal harmony, this Mystery for which the spike of a thistle is worth something, the thorn of a rose is worth something, the heart of a mother is worth something, became involved with the human person as a man; he became a seed in the womb of a woman, of a girl. He became a man, spoke in the town squares, sat at dinner, and they killed him for it." They killed him for this, and they have killed him for it ever since. Because men and women, as open as they are to accepting the ultimate Mystery implicit in the religious sense of which reason is made, as open as they are in front of hypotheses that are formulated more or less poetically or more or less philosophically, they are just as intransigent and intolerant. It is intolerable to conceive that God, the Mystery, has involved himself with the human person by becoming a man, like you and like me; indeed, less than you, less than me, because he reached only the age of thirty-three, while you, any "you" in this room except for a very few, are older than that.

The Mystery involved himself in our existence, he became a protagonist in this history, and it is he who has called us to make us protagonists of history with—*with*—him.

b) After the *Ave, verum Corpus natum de Maria virgine,* we listened to another work by Mozart: the *Kyrie eleison* of the Coronation Mass. "*Kyrie eleison*," "Lord, have mercy." And what a vastly greater impression then penetrated our hearts, if we were attentive and recollected, as we listened to Rachmaninov's *Gospodi pomilui* (*Kyrie eleison* in Russian) from the Mass of Saint John Chrysostom, from the Liturgy of Saint John Chrysostom, which lasted ten minutes (you didn't realize, but it lasted nearly ten minutes, eight minutes to be exact). For this is the most tremendous thing that can be conceived of in the life of humanity: that the protagonists of the message that saves the world—the messengers of that man who allowed himself to be ensnared by the years of his life, who did not want to extend his hand beyond his thirty-three years, except through my own and yours—precisely you and I, I and you, forget him daily. The fundamental betrayal is *forgetfulness*, not remembering, going against our title (*"Memor Domini," "Memores Domini"*) that gives us a claim and defines us in society: *"Memores Domini."*[70]

c) But once the *Kyrie* ended, we heard, again set to music by Mozart, "*Laudate Dominum omnes gentes, collaudate eum omnes populi, quoniam confirmata est super nos misericordia eius*" ("Praise the Lord all you nations, acclaim him all you peoples, for his mercy upon us endures forever" [Psalm 117]). The *Kyrie eleison* thus ends in a "yes" of embrace, like the embrace of the father to the prodigal son (Luke 15:20). Daily, daily am I the prodigal son, as are you, I hope, because the truth of the Lord prevails forever, the plan of the Father is accomplished!

"*Confirmata est super nos misericordia eius*": the plan of the Father is mercy, the impossible word. It should be the first word to be erased from the dictionary, to be scraped from the dictionary, because gladness and joy—the other impossible words—depend upon it: they depend not on our state of mind, but on mercy, on another—on another! From the womb of another we are mysteriously born, from a choir that is mysteriously constituted by another, made by another, which sings enchantingly, despite everything; even the falling leaves are part of this song, and even their rotting becomes positive. It is the victory that faith recognizes: "This is the victory that conquers the world: our faith" (1 John 5:4). The victory of the Mystery, of the Almighty, of the Father, for which the man Jesus, fully aware, first among us all, accepted to die by an unjust murder: "If it is possible, let it be otherwise, but not my will, but yours be done" (Matthew 26:36-46). How many among our own people, before dying, have borne witness before us—through relatives or directly—this "Thy will be done," that his will is mercy, that it is the recomposing of everything, the salvation of everything: "*Omnis creatura bona*," every creature is good and returns to good, and joy is in the heart of the one who accepts this mysterious plan, a plan that seems contradictory and whose destiny, whose end seems unknown, since it is unknown to us—we who feel even what will happen tomorrow to be unknown.

These are the three fundamental factors of the new creature, of the new ontology that historically entered the world. An ontology has entered history; ontology, instead of being at the origin, has pierced the fabric of history, tearing it apart like the veil of the temple when Christ died. But out of this tearing emerged a more beautiful newness: the positivity of everything. Everything is embraced by mercy, everything becomes the prelude to a feast, to that "celestial kingdom, / that fulfills every feast / for which the heart has longed" (I've been repeating this phrase of Jacopone da Todi to myself since ninth grade).[71]

***

In front of this message, what kind of existence is there for us, who have been called? For us, the elect, for us, whom he has grasped and compelled onto this path—for we were compelled, certainly, compelled in such a way that, had we not wanted it, we would have fled. If we did not want this path, we would deny him, because we would have to deny him now, if we did not accept him. What attitude, what morality, what existence is there for the new man, the one who has been called, the one given foresight, the one reached by the proclamation, the one baptized, who has been clothed in Christ, who has become one with Christ (as my body seems to be one with my clothing, according to the Pauline analogy: "clothed with Christ" [Galatians 3:27])? For the new creature, for the new ontology, God became flesh. With every man or woman he chooses, he knocks at the door and he is neither recognized nor accepted. We have recognized him, accepted him: he made himself be recognized, he made himself be accepted. But then, "*Kyrie eleison*," have mercy! Forgetfulness, the forgetfulness that is made ontologically—ontologically!—concrete in sin. But God's mercy is ultimately victorious. The Lord's truth, his plan for the world, prevails for eternity.

God and Man

So then, what are the characteristics of Christian existence, that is, of our behavior and our attitude? Which is our morality, the new morality? *"Fac ut ardeat cor meum in amando Christum Deum ut sibi complaceam"* ("Make my heart burn in loving Christ, so that I may be pleasing to him").[72] Did you hear, last night, the end of the first part of Dvořák's *Stabat Mater*? That continuous repetition of the phrase, which first seems monotonous, but then becomes the most impressive thing in all his music: *"Fac ut ardeat cor meum,"* my whole existence, the totality of existence.

The first characteristic of the new morality is that all of existence is implicated (so that even when you go to the hairdresser, the vision for your hair is born from this; it must be something beautiful and good, however, for the Lord). One cannot avoid this totality. Wherever we jump, we are inside, we are within that embrace; we cannot fasten a button without saying "I offer it to you."

This is the great law: making familiar, almost continuous, or at least evident, this "I offer it to you" in any gesture, because otherwise not a single gesture makes sense. In fact, when one is in despair, he no longer fastens any buttons, he goes around unbuttoned (wherever the button may be!). *"Fac ut ardeat cor meum* [totality] *in amando Christum Deum."* To love is to affirm another: every action affirms him—may every action affirm him! This is life that becomes prayer, the totality of existence that becomes prayer, the affirmation of you: forgetfulness of self and, therefore, finding oneself again in the arms of that great man ("Woman, do not weep!" Luke 7:13).

The only law of life: "Simon, do you love me?" "Yes, Lord, yes." You cannot let too many days pass by without feeling the need to reread that half page of the twenty-first chapter of Saint John's Gospel! *"In amando Christum Deum"* is the only law, no other law exists. The Gospel itself says it, and Saint Paul repeats it: *"In amando Christum Deum ut sibi complaceam,"* so that the outcome of my time, of my energy, the outcome of my breathing, of my being here, of my existing, may be his glory (Colossians 1:10, 2 Corinthians 5:6-9).

Time and the Temple

Along with the twenty-first chapter of Saint John's Gospel, one must always read the first verses of the seventeenth: "Father, the hour has come. Glorify your Son." This is the plan of the Father; this is the will of the Mystery. We know exactly—exactly, like a phrase we heard directly from our father or mother—we know exactly what, for the Mystery, is the *purpose* of all of reality: the glory of his dealings with men and women, of his involvement with men and women, the glory of the Son made man. The glory of the Son made man! It is as if to say: the glory of the Mystery is inexorable, it is like a tank that crushes any resistance, but the glory of the Mystery made man, a man who was the son of a woman... he can be fought against; he can be murdered. So, the Mystery makes him rise again, but he can still be murdered. And the most commonplace murder is the total forgetfulness on the part of those who have known him. What can be said about the forgetfulness of those who have been called to be, with him, protagonists of the Gospel, of the good news—of the fact that the Mystery is good, of the kind face of the Mystery in the world, of the kind face of the Mystery, which is mercy?! "See, I have made a new way. It is already there, do you not perceive it?" (Isaiah 43:19) May the lament of the prophet Isaiah fall within us, let our hearts gather it every morning; every morning, where the darkness launches its attack on the light, where the light must win its place amid the darkness and not settle for twilight.

New times, a new time that the Mystery has allowed to materialize, to be confirmed even by the universal admission of the importance of Christ's birth, so much so that humanity counts its years starting from it: 1995. Certainly, the time will come when the Hegira will cut off many of our heads, just as Christ was murdered![73] But the resurrection is the answer of the omnipotent Mystery to the claim of this world, and the resurrection occurred in this world, in a land: a stone was rolled back and a man appeared in the Upper Room, saying, "Peace be with you." And they were afraid, thinking that they were seeing a ghost. "Peace be with you: give me something to eat, give me something to drink" (Luke 24:36-43). Eat and drink, eat and drink: have you nothing to do

God and Man

but eat and drink? You always eat and drink! All your basic acts are eating and drinking. Exactly! The most inexorably carnal acts.

***

Let us look now in brief detail, as a third point, at the characteristics of the person of these new times, of human existence ("*Fac ut ardeat cor meum in amando Christum Deum ut sibi complaceam*") in an age made new by the presence of the Word made flesh ("*Ave, verum Corpus natum de Maria virgine*") and in which the whole world, albeit unknowingly, cries out praise to God ("*Laudate Dominum omnes gentes*"). I would note these points down as a program for Lent. May they be seeds sown again into the clods of our conscience to defeat its aridity, to defeat its brutal and naturalistic sentimentalism, to defeat the allure, our succumbing to the allure of the fantasies of evil, to a denial of the good.

First. An absolutely new and fascinating sense of self. Whereby I cannot even be held back by all the evil I have done, by all the evil I did today and that I still do. I can never be scandalized by anything of what I have been: everything I did until a moment ago "never existed."[74] It requires the omnipotence of the Mystery to draw reality, the creature, out of nothingness, and it would require the might of the Mystery, the infinite and omnipotent might of the Mystery, to turn into nothingness something that is there. This happens to sin; this happens to my sins: "All this never existed!"

Kierkegaard, once again, incisively draws a conclusion: "Mine is not what belongs to me, but that to which I belong."[75] He does not say, "Mine is not what belongs to me, but what belongs to another," but rather, "Mine is that to which I belong." Things are mine, and people are mine, but I belong-to. Things and people belong, in me, to another—in me, to another. I do not belong to them; this would be the most negative point of view, the most ridiculous and at the same time most shameful and deleterious equivocation. Persons and things, that is, belong to me, not I to them: I belong to you, O Christ. In me, these people and these things belong to you. In me, they belong to you: they are mine, or yours. "Mine is not what belongs to me, but that to which I belong." It might sound like the death of the self, but instead, it is to possess the true life of the self: you are my true life. For that matter, the first miracle, the very first miracle in an absolute sense, is the discovery of the "you." For it is the "you" that brings behind it the scarcely perceptible silhouette of the presence of the infinite, of the eternal, of the man Jesus—the man Jesus.

I want to insist on this point. This new self-awareness is a new subject who enters the world, that is in the world—we are new subjects who enter the world. It is a self-awareness that differs from everyone else's: my "I" is you, everything is mine because I am yours—it is mine because I am yours! This striking detachment, this dizzying reversal, is announced by Saint Paul in his First Letter to the Corinthians, in the seventh chapter: "I tell you, brethren, the time is short. From now on, let those who have wives live as if they had none, those who weep as if they did not weep, and those who rejoice as if they did not rejoice, those who buy as if they did not own, those who use the world as if they did not use it. For indeed, the appearance of this world is passing away" (1 Corinthians 7:29-31). Fr. Eugenio Corecco, you told me last year, as you were leaving your room down that long, narrow corridor: "Time is growing short."[76] For you it has been fulfilled: make our eyes always capable of seeing the brevity of appearances.

Second. This helps us understand better a phrase by the English poet Shelley, which we heard yesterday, but which is much deeper than what we understood yesterday: "We look before and after, / And pine for what is not."[77] We pine because the present has no density, so we look to what comes before and after. As when faced with a temptation: to take, to grasp or not to grasp? Do I take this person as I want him or her, or do I not take as I want? It is a future, it is a tomorrow, it is an after, it is in a minute, it is in a second. If you give in, when you take the person, you are dissatisfied—so much so that you grit your teeth, you helplessly clutch at a thing that escapes between your hooklike fingers, you bite at a thing that escapes your teeth. "We look before and after, / And pine for what is not." There is only the you. What is there is only the you, the you of being, of which that person is an expression. And the sacrilege that I commit in biting with my teeth, in grasping with my hands, even with the hands and teeth of my imagination, this sacrilege that I commit reveals that what I have been expecting from the "after" is not in the present anymore, it is already no longer in the present.

Third. In the Letter to Diognetus, in the year 150, the Christian author writes, "They have among themselves a respect inconceivable to others."[78] The Christians have among themselves a respect that is inconceivable to others. "Respect" comes from the Latin *respicio*, which means to look at something while being aware, out of the corner of one's eye, of something else. What is seen out of the corner of the eye is different from what dominates the focus of observation. *Respicio*, respect: looking at a person or a thing while being aware of another that dominates from the horizon, like the sun. The sun is always in the corner of the eye and focuses our eye on everything.

These three things, then: a new self-awareness in which not what I possess, but what I belong to, is mine; the inexorable dissatisfaction of the instant in which you grasp, in which you would grasp; "a capacity for respect unknown to others," a respect for the person, a respect for the other, dominated by that other figure. I fix my gaze and my heart on you, but on the ultimate horizon, kept present in the corner of my eye, another figure illuminates you, another figure gives you life, gives you flesh, gives you bones, gives you existence: you are mine because you belong to another, and because I belong to another. Only in this way, in fact, do I belong to another: by accepting that you belong to another. By recognizing that you belong to another, I belong to another.

***

Allow me an observation. Sin is ugly. Transience is ugly. No sooner do you say, "How beautiful!" than it is already gone. Therefore, it is deception, and deception prevails over the impression of beauty. If you remember what is beautiful about it, if you evoke what is beautiful, you have to make an effort yourself; you evoke something that you create, or recreate. You recreate in imagination what was not in existence. Sin is ugly; it is as ugly as deception. A beautiful thing, used for deception, kills you. Here, again, returns the echo of the "time grows short" from the First Letter to the Corinthians.

As we read in a saying of the Desert Fathers, "A brother questioned Abbot Poemen and said to him, 'My father, when a brother dwells with me, where do you want me to look?' He said to him, 'Put your sins on his head and look at them.'"[79] Killing the other is ugliness, an ugliness made by you, not in the creature, who is good. "'My father, when a brother dwells with me, where do you want me to look?' He said to him, 'Put your sins on his head and look at them.'"

But it is actually a novice of the very first year, who has just entered the house, who gives us a sharp lesson on the chronological and physiological origin of evil, of sin: "Today," she writes in a letter, "I was thinking that a lack of faith is never with respect to the declarations we make of belief in Jesus Christ as a theoretical formulation [theoretically, Jesus Christ is Jesus Christ; it is difficult for there to be someone among us who puts this in doubt]; but we lack faith all the times that we do not believe in his promise, that is, in the experience of good that we have." We lack faith every time we do not believe in the promise of the hundredfold here below, of the new man or woman and the hundredfold here below, that is, every time we do not believe in "the experience of the good that we have": if he is present, he changes us. We do not believe in that change as something both possible and already happening. This applies to us all: no matter which of you I might approach, I am likely to find a certain discouragement, because you do not believe in the good that you already do, that you otherwise would not have done. It is as if that were something to tolerate, even to

God and Man

endure, so greatly is the root of desire strained toward something else, toward the ephemeral and deceitful.

"And so long," the letter continues, "as they remain moral precepts to follow [respect for the person, denial of deception, resistance against the negative and equivocal imagination], as long as they remain moral precepts to follow everything is fine." It's beautiful! This description of the new man is beautiful. "But when Jesus [slicing through these figures with a sword] declares that he loves me very much, so much that he would lay down his life for me, and that he desires me so much that he will always forgive me [that he desires me so much that he will always forgive me!], then, in that moment, what seems like a simple reservation about concrete existence, a reservation that is easily understood [due to our weakness], turns out, in time, to be the place of a 'no.'"

This being uncertain, this being dissatisfied with the good that we do, that we never would have done otherwise—because it is Christ who gives us this new consistency of self-awareness, this new sense of the other, this new dramatic sense of possession, because what is mine is mine because I am another's—generates a reluctance: "but who knows, who knows!" One does not say, "I am dissatisfied," as one would if one were sincere, but, "I am not persuaded, it does not convince me." This reluctance (here the word "reluctance" is absolutely right), which is not denial, this reluctance which is understandable because of our weakness, becomes, in time, if it lasts through time, the place of a "no."[80] One does not say "no" openly against God who became man, against Christ and Christ crucified; one does not say "no" to Christmas or to Easter. And yet, look at how you live in the house! Christ has nothing to do with it. The house, then, has no meaning except that of a hotel with friends, a friendly hotel, where we can demand, above all where we can demand, from which we can expect everything to be done for us and where we can demand something that we seem to lack; I need it and you give it to me! The "no," as is very shrewdly stated a little further on in the letter, the "no" is to the instruments that Jesus uses to reach us. It is not to him, it is to the tools (that a girl of her age should understand these things!): "What seems like a simple reservation ... turns out, in time, to be the place of a 'no,' a real lack of faith toward the witness who meets me in the name of Christ. And so, this very easy reservation is revealed to be a real impediment to the love of Christ, to the possibility of experiencing him." If you bring me the message—his presence—through your experience, if you bring it to me, I experience it; if you do not bring it to me, I do not experience it, it is merely an idea I can read in books, it is a theoretical formulation. Therefore, if the house is no longer the source of the experience of him, what attraction can it have? (It could be attractive if there were a girl there, if there were girls there as well, but even in that regard you are freer outside.)

"Because," the letter continues, "Doubting this [the reservation of before], if I prevent myself from believing in the way and the place [you see what amazing logic!], if I prevent myself [she reiterates] from giving credit to the way and the place in which he says he comes to me [in which Jesus says he comes: 'I come through the house, I come through the friend, I come through the *Memores Domini*'], how else should I wait for him?" How else? If I stop myself from believing in the way and the place in which he says he comes—and he tells you this because the others tell you, the house tells you, the *Memores Domini* tells you—how else should I wait for him? In a dream of mine? I can see right away that any other expectation is a dream of mine. "I have tried to answer this question, but from the only alternative is an attempt of the imagination. This is where abstraction begins." A vocation is a life that has been given; if a vocation becomes abstraction, it is impossible to live it, it is an absurdity! Because life is the thing most contrary to abstraction that exists—this is why philosophers do not understand life and poets must imagine it differently.

The opposite of this reluctance, what prevents what this girl called "reluctance"—which is a reluctance toward Jesus because it is toward those through whom he came to me; it is a reluctance toward the place of the well from which I drew in the beginning— is a surge of "surrender." This surge of "surrender" tears you away, detaches you from what you are; it is such a rush that it is as if you leave your clothes behind: you are left naked—that is, poor. Poor:

you don't care if the others laugh, if the others are scandalized, if the others equivocate. If the others laugh, are scandalized and equivocate, it doesn't matter to you! It is a surge of surrender that is called "poverty," or more accurately, whose imposing, existential outcome is poverty. It doesn't seem like it, but love of poverty, the overt acceptance of poverty, is an indication that reluctance is not there, an indication that this surge of surrender is there. Real poverty concerning cars, money, telephones, clothes, theaters, televisions, whatever you want, everything on which you offload what you seem to not have, on which you offload the desire for what you seem to lack, and thus, "What I had grasped, longing, / in my clenched hands fell apart,"[81] in hooklike hands it fell apart ("Where are you going?" "I'm going out." He is going to the movies. Yes, for the love of God, go to the movies as much as you want, but don't stop me from giving you dirty looks when you get home. I know it depends on the movie! One in a thousand. One in a thousand may be spared. The proportion, these days, is not much greater). Either entering into relationship with things and people is an act of desiring to know the beauty of Christ, the truth of Christ, to have compassion for the condemnation of Christ, or it is a way to participate in the condemnation of the world and its ultimately intended murder. Because the world is murderous—see the last two lines of the first chapter of the Book of Wisdom: "Man pines for death." The world is, by its very nature, ultimately murderous.

We have stated, then, both the characteristics of the new ontology and the features of a new existence: "*Fac ut ardeat cor meum in amando Christum Deum.*" The change of mentality from the Middle Ages to the modern age lies entirely in the different interpretation of this tercet of the Stabat Mater: the "*Fac ut ardeat cor meum in amando Christum Deum*" is repugnant to the person of today, it is abhorrent, because it seems like an abstraction that takes all of life, that becomes a rule of life. Instead, it is not so! It is a new self-awareness, in which the true "I" lies in being possessed by Christ; it is a new respect for the person, unknown to others; it is the density of the moment, the present, the pure present, which is the substantial moment: which does not send you back to yesterday, which is not beautiful because it makes you think of yesterday or of the next instant. It is the victory that the surge of surrender, of adherence to him, achieves over the malignant reluctance, over the serpent of reluctance, who does not say, "God does not exist," but "If you eat the fruit, you will be like God," if you eat the fruit, you will be happy (Genesis 3:4-5).

This whole list of things constitutes a new people, which can be identified according to what Saint Augustine says in the *De civitate Dei*: "*Ut videatur qualis quisque populus sit illa sunt intuenda quae diligit*":[82] in order to see what kind of people it is (what kind of house it is, what kind of *Memores Domini* group it is, what kind of Christianity it is), one must gaze upon, discover, intuit (*intuenda*[83]) the things it loves. What you love defines you. Saint Thomas says, "Man's life consists in the affection which principally sustains him and in which he finds his greatest satisfaction." This is the criterion that defines a people. A people: a man and a woman who marry, a family, a house of the *Memores Domini*, a convent of friars, a monastery of monks. A people like that of the Middle Ages or a people like that of the fifteenth century, the sixteenth, the seventeenth, the eighteenth, the nineteenth, the twentieth, or of the year two thousand, which is as de-christianized as when Christ came—as when Christ came!—and we are at the level of the "yes" of Saint Peter, we are at the level of the wonder of Andrew and John, at that level. If we are at that level, with all the sins we carry along, we are living the covenant, we are living the promise, and "whoever has this hope in him, purifies himself as he is pure" (1 John 3:3).

A friend of ours gives us the rule that we must take home with us, a recommendation that you must take home with you. It comes from the Desert Fathers: "Apply yourself to doing good, and do not fear your weakness."[84] I add: "in good times and in bad," as the marriage rite says. This can be seen in the present. This defines the present: "Apply yourself to doing good." The first good is recognizing Jesus, without reserve. "Do not fear your weakness":

whether the circumstance is favorable or unfavorable. The present, the present time, the present moment, is the verification.

"I have sought you in the sanctuary, to behold your strength and your glory" (Psalm 63:3). "I have sought you in the sanctuary." In the place where you have chosen to communicate yourself, I have sought you: in the house, in the *Memores Domini*, in the movement, in the Church. "I have sought you in the sanctuary, to behold your strength and your glory": if I were not weak, you would not be powerful, I would not know that you are powerful, I would not know what it means that you are powerful. And to acknowledge this is so profoundly your glory that it becomes my own joy. "The glory of God is the living man," a man in joy, in the fullness of life, in joy.[85] "For your grace is worth more than life" (Psalm 63:4). Let us repeat it together, slowly: "For your grace is worth more than life."

The things we have said are important, and true, in order to live; we are nothing, poor people in the worst sense of the word, poor worms, if we do not listen to these words.

4

The Subject in Time and in the Temple: The I

"*HIC DIES, IN QUO tibi consecratum conspicis Templum, tribuat perenne gaudium nobis, vigeatque longo Temporis usu*": "May this day, on which you look upon the Temple consecrated to you, grant us everlasting joy, and may it remain strong through the long use of time."[86] May this day on which you look upon the Temple consecrated to you—a day of retreat, a day of spiritual exercises, an hour of silence a day: this is the time when the mystery of the Father looks upon the temple consecrated to him—may this time grant us perpetual joy and remain strong—strong: a strong day, a strong time—remain strong for our use, for our life, over a long span of time. May it remain strong for the concrete existence of our life and for a long span of time, which is the dream of every life (thank goodness that this is not the ultimate purpose of life, but nevertheless it is what we dream of).

"*Hic dies, in quo tibi consecratum conspicis Templum, tribuat perenne gaudium nobis, vigeatque longo Temporis usu*": when it falls to you to sing this penultimate stanza of the hymn, the eleventh stanza of the hymn we sing to Christ at every meeting of the house, reflect on the humanity into which divinity translates itself.[87]

The Subject in Time and in the Temple: The I

And there is yet another idea that you must emphasize. It is not meant to be a summary of all this grace-filled time in which the Lord dictated the previous three lessons to us,[88] but rather a continuation of that wonderful time, which was a grace of the Spirit as long and deep as a vast lake on the barren land of our hearts. What he said to us in this time cannot be summarized by what I will say today. My words today simply intend to existentialize all that has been said, and all that has been said becomes existential in a placeless place, in a spiritual place. It is a place, however, that is made of earth and of flesh, which is spiritual because it is also made of soul: the "I." It is in the "I" that everything that has been said is existentially realized. Here, here, are the four walls; here is the temple; here is the concrete place of the vocation; here are the blessed waters that dissolve the sins of those who committed them, and they perish, they become nothing: "All this never happened."[89] "*Genus et creatur Christicolarum*" ("you form a Christian people") and, at the same time, the Spirit—*chrismate invictum* ("unconquered through anointing")—the Spirit creates a new *gens*, a new *genus*, a new kind of creature, who is more than a man: *genus "Christicolarum*," the lineage of those who recognize, adore, hope in, and love Christ; believe in Christ, hope in Christ, love Christ: "Peter, do you love me?"—You!—"Yes, Lord, I love you."

This synthesis, which we allude to in the brief but weighty remarks we will make today, is to be taken up by all of us, one by one, to grow in knowledge of ourselves and to perceive where we are, at what point we are—not as a measure but as a horizon. You stop in the desert road or in the flourishing road that you are traveling, in the sad or the joyful road that you are traveling, you stop and look at the horizon: you do not measure what you have accomplished, you do not measure what is left, you look at the horizon, which is Christ.

Two small considerations.

First. As mentioned in a brief intervention yesterday, when faced with the question: "Why are we unable to bear the time it takes to construct the road, until the road is built? Why can't we bear the time?" The answer is that one does not build unless one says, "I follow one who is alive." I follow; I seek one who is alive. "Seek out daily the faces of the saints and draw comfort from their words," Fr. Villa taught us, writing them on the walls of his house and filling the house of the Curia with light (whereas before there was darkness).[90] "I follow one who is alive. So, I stay with him—certainly, one who is alive . . . so I stay with him!—and I try to become one with him." It is not an exaggeration. It is a definition and applies, therefore, to every relationship that is genuine, that is undertaken authentically. "I follow one who is alive. So, I stay with him and I try to become one with him." This phrase, too, reduces the conditions for living the vocation to the bare minimum of simplicity.

Let us carefully enumerate what the word *alive* means.

1. In one of our houses it was said: "Recognize Christ as the presence that constitutes us." This is the act of faith. Living means that one lives the faith, that one recognizes Christ as the presence that constitutes us. To recognize Christ as the presence that constitutes us: this is why he is the proper object of memory, whereby this presence reconstitutes itself to constitute me anew.

The contribution continues: "This Christ whom you are—this Christ whom you are!—why does he get up in the morning?" Why does he go to work? Why, in general does he act? For what does he act? Or rather, what does he await from all that moves him and that propels him into the future? "Our rightfully contented life, which is satisfied up to a certain point, cannot be *intense*," it cannot be intense with the intensity that Maspes demanded in that unforgettable summation of his, when he wrote in a letter, speaking of the present moment: "the density of the instant."[91] "Our rightfully contented life, which is even satisfied up to a certain point, cannot be intense, dense, without this question being answered." Why did Christ come in the womb of Mary? Why did Christ live in his house in Nazareth? Why did Christ move to go work in his father's workshop and in the great workshop of the Father—with a capital F—which were the streets of Judea, Galilee, Samaria, Jerusalem?

"It is as if we were missing something, which is the outcome of our commitment, the outcome of the gift that we are." And it is this "something" that is missing that, in spite of everything, sustains the gift that we are, it sustains our efforts; it gives us the reason, the reason for time and space, the reason that is commensurate to the history of humankind, proportionate with the history of humankind. Christ came to do all this, to give his life as the salvation of the person: *propter nos homines*.[92] "It is as if our life were a fetus whose head had not yet formed." Without the response that we have given to Christ, it is as if our life were a fetus whose head had not yet formed. Hope when confronting the present is the fulfillment of the present, the realization of the present, the complete realization of satisfaction—hope driven by passion for the world, yearning because men and women do not know Christ or, to formulate it more lovingly, because Christ is not recognized by them.

Because Christ is not recognized by men and women, this is why we get up in the morning, and go to work, and say our first words to each other—say words that are stammered at first, strained at first, then become increasingly fluent, and always more eager to win over the people with whom we work. Then we come home tired and go back to rest so that the next day it can all happen again.

The reason is because Christ is not recognized. So this love, full of longing for Christ and for others and for their destiny, becomes a hope for the present, a present that begins as faith, as becoming aware of his presence, as becoming aware of the presence that constitutes me and that is not recognized by men and women, it is not recognized! All the hope of my life, all the expectation of my life, what engulfs all that I do—all that I do, because it is in action that the present becomes a hope for the future—is so that they might know him, that all may know him: this is the aching hope that fulfills the faith and charity of the one who is alive. The first characteristic of the living person is, therefore, faith according to the pattern of its unfolding, hope and longing for Christ and for men and women (2 Corinthians 5:14 ff.).

2. But there is a second characteristic, still mysterious, within this mysterious "I"....

For what is the "I" that you hold in your hand, under your fingers, under your eyes that gaze at it, with your heart throbbing or remaining in suspense without knowing what to say? This "I," which in any case quivers under your fingers, under your eyes that gaze at it, and awakens in your heart certain overtones that are the overtones of life, this "I," if you first look at it as a believer, recognizes that Christ is its substance, recognizes Christ as the presence that constitutes it. And having recognized Christ as the presence that constitutes it, the "I" is immediately bent over, it tends to bend over with yearning because Christ is not recognized, and out of pity for men and women, as sign and symbol of the pity for oneself.

But this "I"—I was saying—has another mysterious aspect, which is the one emphasized by Saint Augustine, as we read the first evening: "We are not exhorted not to love [we are not exhorted not to love: whoever does not love is dead!], but to choose the object of our love. But how can we choose if we are not first *chosen* [if love is not shown to us, when we are first given life]? For we cannot love unless we are first loved. Listen to John the Apostle: 'We love because he first loved us.'"[93]

3. The third characteristic of a living man or woman—because it would be worth nothing for one to have as much faith as you could imagine, to be chosen by all the angels who came down from heaven precisely to cry out in the cathedral square that he had been chosen, if he were not first of all humanly certain—certain! "For we recognize the Lord whom no creature is able to resist."[94] There is one among us whom no creature can resist. And the miracles of holiness mark the history of this event in its sharpest points, at its highest ridges, establishing the chain of mountains that it creates.

Certain! Certainty is an indispensable condition for liveliness; especially for a liveliness that must impose itself as hope, and therefore as consolation and therefore as joy in the eyes of our

The Subject in Time and in the Temple: The I

brethren. My God, how necessary is this summons to inevitable certainty! We who tremble, who tremble more than we believe, who, full of doubt, bury ourselves in our "who knows?"

This is why you will go read the first part of the eighteenth chapter of the Gospel of Saint Luke. But why should I say to you, "You will go and read it"? A meditation dictated to others can also be a meditation for the one who dictates it. So:

> He told them a parable about the need to pray always without growing weary [because the living "I" is the one who is certain, certain because she prays, asks, begs; her strength lies in begging]. "There was in a city a judge who neither feared God nor respected any human being. In that city there was also a widow who would go to him and say, 'Grant me justice against my adversary.' For a time he was unwilling, but then he thought to himself, 'While I neither fear God nor respect any human being [as is the case with many administrators of justice], because this widow is so troublesome, I will do her justice so that she will not come and harass me continually.'" And the Lord added, "Did you hear what the dishonest judge said? [To avoid being bothered, let us give her satisfaction at once.] And will not God do justice to his elect who cry out to him day and night? Will he make them wait long? I tell you, he will do justice to them promptly [he will give them certainty, a capacity for certainty, promptly]. But when the Son of Man comes, will he find faith on earth?" (Luke 18:1-8).

We say we are "not of the world," we say this about ourselves when we partake more of the world than of the presence by which we have been constituted. We are more of the world than of Christ! Our memory indicates this, it indicates it very well: look at the outline of our memory.

A living person, therefore, is first of all a person of faith: Christ is the presence that constitutes me. And this "I" constituted by him is such because it has been chosen: the root of truth in me is that I am chosen. And this fact, when we become aware of it, floods us with certainty. Certainty: this is the most evident aspect of one who is alive. For such a one, God is truly the Father, he is everything; prior to the Father there is nothing, there is only the void.

And if Jesus, of whom we are constituted, is he whom no creature is able to resist—as Saint Ephraim says—then what do we have to fear? If we look at him, if we follow him, if we beg him, if we follow him with a beggar's gaze as the apostles followed him, if we follow him with that hunger and thirst for justice that he kindled within the heart, if we follow him like that, what do we have to fear, if no creature is capable of overcoming him?

And no creature is able to resist him because "every house is built by someone," as the Letter to the Hebrews says: "Every house is built by someone, but the builder of all is God" (Hebrews 3:4). Hence, he is the Lord, the Father and Lord; the Father, because we are dealing with a home, the Father.

But precisely because we are dealing with something infinitely new—Christ is the presence that constitutes me—I am another being, I don't understand how, but I am another being: chosen, why have I been chosen? Chosen from among an infinite number of possibilities—infinite!—and chosen endlessly, with a certainty that is rooted in an inexhaustible depth, and, even before that, limitless, without measure. And this certainty ends at the shore of a horizon that is the source of all this endlessness, the source of all this mystery: a force that nothing can resist. This is revealed in Christ, in whose hands the Father has placed everything, to whose hands the Father has given everything—everything! (John 3:35). And the meaning of all the smallest invisible things, every infinitesimal thing, and the meaning of the greatest things is him, it is him, and he will appear, he will appear! But the origin of all this mystery is the Father, who has constituted everything: everything depends on the Father. Christ himself, the word he most repeated in his three years of public life, the word heard most often by all, that echoed most in the hearts of the apostles is "The Father": "I always do what pleases the Father," always (John 8:29).

The Subject in Time and in the Temple: The I

4. This Mystery, which constitutes me and which I have discovered, constitutes all things—but above all it constitutes the present in which my future resides, in which my future, my destiny, is shaped, in which my destiny is shaped and affirmed. But how does one make contact with this mystery, how does one know with certainty that one has been chosen, so much as to be constituted by it? How does one know this and become aware of it, and understand it more and more? By being in a place, by staying in a place that has similarly been chosen.

"A brother who was haunted by the thought of leaving the monastery opened up to me. So I replied, 'Stay in your cell, pledge your body to the four walls of your cell. Do not worry about that thought: let the thought go where it wants [let it come when it wants, and go where it wants], but do not let your body leave the cell.'"[95] What absolute simplicity, what banality! We are all tempted—all of us!—to say: "What a banality: that my destiny, my identification of my vocation and the meaning of my life, are marked out by the four walls in which I find myself, the four walls of the circumstances of time and space, the four walls of the history in which he made me find myself."

A living person is one who believes, who is aware of having been chosen, who is certain of the Father who is everything—of the Father who is perceived, grasped, adored, and loved in the place where you are, where he has placed you: within the four walls, which, if these four walls were the galaxies of the universe, would remain four walls because they would still be defined by a finite relationship. Four walls: to stay in a place without those unstable and questionable interpretations that we prop up with our own thoughts and our own imagination. This place has nothing to do with imagination or thought. It is about the thought at its root, which is awareness of a reality, and about the heart, which loves and adheres to this reality—nothing more.

I seek those who live, and I stay close to them and even try to become one with them: "Do you not know that you are members of each other?" (Romans 12:5).

Second. Yesterday's intervention continues, "To build, it is not enough to last through time—one must give life." It is necessary to give life as you have received life, it is necessary that through you, others receive life. But is this possible? It is necessary that through you, others be called, others be chosen, others believe: this is the mission of your life, the answer to the great question that we talked about earlier.

These are the same two points from the summary of our exercises.[96] To be a missionary means to give life to a people, sent by Christ, sent by Christ as Christ is sent by the Father. Christ is sent by the Father to regenerate humanity, a new humanity, a different humanity, one that gathers together all the hints and efforts of the first humanity and transforms them, changing their nature, their value, to a nature similar to that of God. Without this impetus, without this yearning, it is as if faith itself no longer mattered. Faith cannot give you joy if it does not stir up this yearning. For one without missionary passion—anyone, I am not speaking about our friends who go to Nazareth or our friends who go to the distant lands of Siberia, I am speaking about each one of us—it is as if your body were without seed—that is, sterile—and your breast without a heart—that is, arid. Your thought and your understanding do not reach the *affectus*, they are not moved, they cannot be moved. You are barren, barren in the shameful sense that women of certain cultures—not only ancient ones—live in the eyes of others if they are childless.

What gives life to a new people, what contributes to the generation of a new people? What is the lament of a people that forms the most decisive expression in the literary history of humanity, the expressive power of lamenting what is missing from life? The psalms, the singing of the psalms, this long lament of Jewish history. Go and read Psalm 10, Psalm 88, Psalm 111, and Psalm 124; these psalms are among those chosen for the breviary from the last two weeks. But we read these things without resonating with them, we say these words as if they were not our own, indeed, as if they were nobody's, the Nobody of *The Odyssey*: "Who are you?" "Nobody."[97]

The Subject in Time and in the Temple: The I

And the people that walks in search of its destiny and its fulfillment, in addition to the song of lament, that is ultimately a lament—for even from its notes of greatest certainty it lapses into sorrowful lamentation—this people also has the voice of its poets, its geniuses: genius, that which expresses the consciousness of the people, which expresses the genius of the people.[98] In the Bible they are called prophets: see Isaiah 2:2-5, Isaiah 66:10-14, and above all Isaiah 61:10-62:7 (the verses that form the climax of these chapters).

If in these two weeks we have not resonated and wept with the Jewish people, if we have not felt on us and within us, within our existence, the pain of the Jewish people, if we have not relived the history of this people, then the Event of Christ is not present for us, the Event does not exist; we have lived as if the Event did not exist.

How rightly, then, we specify that the figure of the living person is to be followed closely, so as to be united in one: "Do you not know that you are members of each other?"

1. The objectivity of the form of the vocation saves this living closeness, for this loving and generous closeness is recognized as an echo of the heart of Christ. Objectivity: the four walls that make the path simple. As simple as this: "Stay where you are," stay where you are. The pointing out of your path is so simple, it makes the way simple, it gets rid of all recriminations—oh how wonderful this is! Recrimination is the satanic and demonic encumbrance of our days, which would otherwise be more serene: even if it is raining and the clouds are low and black, the soul can be serene by drinking in the air of the Spirit that runs between the drops of the falling rain. The objectivity of the vocation gets rid of all recriminations and therefore all useless labor, leaving the only reasonable toil, which is that of bearing witness, of mission, of dedicating oneself to the mission of Christ. Thus, the whole vision of the living person's engagement with life remains simple.

2. And *free*: the person who lives is free. Free from what? Free from everything that was; this is why he is untouched by any

recrimination, because recrimination revives what was. He is free from himself, that is, from what he once was; free in what is now, in Christ who is now, in the presence of Christ that he recognizes, in the presence of Christ recognized as his own—his own!—only consistency; free from the chains of time and space; and free in relationships. That a relationship perceptibly liberates you, this is the mark of its authenticity and its goodness: that it liberates you, not that it complicates you, binds you, weighs and drags you down, or determines you.

3. As a consequence of this simplicity and freedom, the living person is capable of joy. Capable of joy: a reflection of the sky, of the starry sky, of the blue sky of springtime, "cold but burning."[99]

4. And therefore the living person—who from simplicity and freedom draws the capacity for joy—is a desirable person. Desirability is a characteristic of those who are free; desirability is a characteristic of those who are sent. Sent to whom? To the wayfarer, to all the wayfarers; not to the wanderers, not to those who refuse to be wayfarers. Not to those who refuse to have a way, a destiny, and a companionship—which is mysterious but given to them with certainty—and prefer instead to make of themselves their own path and their own destiny. Not for the vagabonds, but for the wayfarers. For the wayfarers, joy and desirability form the background of the presence of the person who has been chosen, who has faith in Jesus. And if one is far away, one desires this from afar. One desires the place where the free person lives. One yearns for that place, with a nostalgia in the true sense of the word: it makes you hasten to finish what you have to do while you are away, and breathe again when you take up the means of returning to that original place.[100] Like last night, when I suddenly found myself near one of you who has been obliged to be away for a while these days, and he hugged me with tears in his eyes and said, "No, it's because I'm happy." How many years have we known each other, and he has never done that before! This is the nostalgia for the place, the four walls, where you stay to remain with those who are alive, those

who are thrown into a yearning passion that Christ be recognized, that their faith be communicated—thrown, that is, into mission. "I am Mañara, the one who lies when he says, 'I love.' But because I told the Eternal One that I loved him, my heart is joyful and my hands are desirable as loaves of bread." Desirability. "I am Mañara. And he whom I love tells me, 'All these things never were.' If you have stolen, if you have killed, let these things never have been. He alone is."[101] We must read this whole passage from *Miguel Mañara*, thinking of the example that our friends in Nazareth have given us and continue to give us—our three companions who are sharing a common life, living the experience of a house in Nazareth.

> Dearest Fr. Giussani, a warm greeting and Happy Easter from the house in Nazareth. At Christmas one of us returned [that is, went away, back to Italy]. That dramatic moment presented us with an inescapable position: awaiting the energy of our engagement with reality only from the coming of Christ, putting ourselves totally into play through offering our lives in an entreaty to his mercy to have pity on us and give us his help. In our suffering and bewilderment, we were asked to place our trust in his initiative, to abandon every plan of our own in order to obey—and first and foremost in our daily work to obey the Prior [of the local convent of friars. These three friends of ours are so far from us, so different from us, but by no means so far or so different that we cannot admire how they live, the awareness with which they live, the precision with which they live their prayers, their fraternal relationships, and their mundane daily work]. We discovered that we were here to build inside the hospital a visible relationship of unity and friendship with the communities of the friars and sisters [not just among us, but with the communities of the friars and sisters], loving them just as they are, and affirming this love in front of everyone. And this task demanded, before anything else, a personal change of ours. To our surprise, we awoke again and rediscovered that what you tell us truly changes the being of our lives. Your words convey the value of real personal change. The arrival of Gualtiero

comforted us with the certainty that we are lovingly guided so that we may learn to live an experience that renews us through embracing one another and accepting every situation. At work, we built an organizational chart and tackled inventory, budget planning, and cost cutting, laying the groundwork for effective management of the Fatebenefratelli Hospital. We have forged relationships with local authorities and health institutions [that is, Jewish ones]. At the same time, we began a School of Community with an Arab family from Nazareth.[102] We were invited to the parish to give a witness and to begin meeting the young people. There is attention and a request for the presence of our experience here, a request to know who we are, from many people.[103] We wait and work with joy for the further development of this dramatic—but real and beautiful—beginning, especially because we realize more and more personally that there is no division between our life at home, our work, the movement, and our being in the world; everything is part of the continuous discovery of our vocation [see how alive they are!]. We always call you to mind before Our Lady each time we go to the grotto of the Annunciation and to the house of Saint Joseph. We experience their real help every day. Going there to see that place makes us living memories of the Event that was generated there by a "yes" like Peter's, the "yes" of Mary. It is through our own "yes," in which echo those of Peter and Our Lady, that the Annunciation, the announcement of the Great Event, remains present.

I was planning on giving a summary of everything that we have said from last August as it pertains to our existence. The three texts—"God: the temple and time," "Recognizing Christ," and "God and Man"—all lead back to one word: "I." This "I" is your existence, my existence, our existence. And to it is entrusted everything that the Father wants from the universe: the glory of Christ. But to feel this, it is not enough to just conform out of sterile obedience—sterile in the sense of lacking the Spirit. One must instead realize that Christ is the Presence that constitutes you, that constitutes the world: "In him all things consist."[104] His glory, that everyone recognize who he is, that everyone recognize what he is for the whole of human reality, for the whole of history: this must be our passionate purpose. Then everything we have said this year will make sense. For these three friends of ours, the house has become much more than what most of you feel the house to be—and with fewer speeches than those given to us. The four walls of the Desert Fathers of fifteen hundred years ago ... suddenly realizing that others have gone before us in something we thought of as a discovery of our own, this is the most beautiful thing there is!

That is why the grace we must ask of Our Lady—and Mass will be said for this intention today—is an ever-greater certainty. Because certainty is what shatters the uncertainty of the world, what establishes the mountains and does not let us tremble amid the most disastrous earthquakes (Psalm 46). As the psalms say: the psalms are the lament of a people who does not yet have this Presence. Just as the prophets are the voices of the poets who feel the imaginative appeal of that for which this people is made, and which has not yet turned itself into bread to eat and wine to drink. For us, in a few minutes, this Presence will translate himself into bread to eat and wine to drink. But we will understand it—in the etymological sense of the word—we will comprehend it, embrace it, or else, even in us, it will remain outside of us.[105]

Appendix

CHRISTE, CUNCTORUM DOMINATOR ALME

In Dedicatione Ecclesiae Maioris Hymnus

Christe, cunctorum dominator alme,
Mente supremi generate Patris,
Supplicum voces pariterque carmen
Cerne benignus.

Cerne, quod Templi Deus, ad decorum
Plebs tua supplex resonet per Ædem,
Annuo cuius redeunt colenda
Tempore festa.

Hæc Domus surgit tibi dedicate
Rite, ubi sumit populus sacratum
Corpus ex aris, bibit et beati
Sanguinis haustum.

Hic sacrosancti latices nocentum
Diluunt culpas, perimuntque noxas;
Chrismate invictum genus et creatur
Christicolarum.

Hic salus ægris, medicina fessis
Lumen et cæcis datur; hic reatu,
Christe, nos solvis, timor atque mæror
Pellitur omnis.

Time and the Temple

Dæmonis sævi perit hic rapina:
Pervicax monstrum pavet, et retentos
Deserens artus, fugit in remotas
Ocius auras.

Hic locus Regis vocitatur Aula
Nempe cælestis, rutilansque cæli
Porta, quæ vitæ Patriam petentes
Accipit omnes.

Turbo quem nullus quatit, aut vagantes
Diruunt venti penetrantque nimbi;
Hanc Domum tetris piceus tenebris
Tartarus horret.

Ergo te votis petimus, sereno
Annuas vultu, famulos gubernes,
Qui tui summo celebrant amore
Gaudia templi.

Nulla nos vitæ cruciet procella;
Sint dies læti placidæque noctes;
Nullus ex nobis, pereunte mundo,
Sentiat ignem.

Hic dies in quo tibi consecratum
Conspicis Templum, tribuat perenne
Gaudium nobis, vigeatque longo
Temporis usu.

Laus poli summum resonet Parentem,
Laus Patris Natum, pariterque Sanctum
Spiritum dulci moduletur hymno
Omne per ævum. Amen.

Appendix

CHRIST, THE KIND RULER OF ALL

Hymn for the Dedication of a Greater Church

O Christ, Lord of all,
Begotten of the mind of the supreme Father,
Graciously look upon our voices in supplication and in song.

See, O God, that to the beauty of your Temple,
The supplication of your people resounds within it,
Whose annual festivals return to be worshiped
In season.

This House rises dedicated to you
Rightly, where the people receive the sacred
Body from the altars, and drink the draught
Of the blessed Blood.

Here the most holy waters wash away
Sin and stain;
Through anointing, you form an unconquered
Christian people.

Here is health for the sick, medicine for the weary,
Light is given to the blind; here, O Christ,
You free us from guilt, and all fear and sorrow
Are driven away.

The wiles of the fierce demon perish here:
The beastly monster fears,
His power restrained, and swiftly flees
Into the distant winds.

This place is called the Hall of the King,
For it is the heavenly, and the shining gate of heaven
Which all who seek the Homeland of life
It receives.

Time and the Temple

A whirlwind which no one shakes, nor do wandering
Winds or penetrating storms destroy;
At this House the dark pitch-black shadows
Of Tartarus shudder.

Therefore we ask you with our prayers, may
Your serene face govern your servants,
Who celebrate with the greatest love
The joys of your Temple.

May no storm of life distress us;
May days be glad and nights serene;
May none of us, when the world passes away,
Feel the fire.

May this day on which you look upon the
Temple consecrated to you, grant us
Everlasting joy, and may it remain strong through long
Use of time.

Let praise resound to the highest Creator of heaven,
Praise to the Father and the Son, and likewise the Holy
Spirit be sung in sweet hymn
Throughout all ages. Amen.

Appendix

STABAT MATER

Stabat mater dolorosa
iuxta Crucem lacrimosa,
dum pendebat Filius.

Cuius animam gementem,
contristatam et dolentem
pertransivit gladius.

O quam tristis et afflicta
fuit illa benedicta,
mater Unigeniti!

Quae maerebat et dolebat,
pia Mater, dum videbat
nati poenas inclyti.

Quis est homo qui non fleret,
matrem Christi si videret
in tanto supplicio?

Quis non posset contristari
Christi Matrem contemplari
dolentem cum Filio?

Pro peccatis suae gentis
vidit Iesum in tormentis,
et flagellis subditum.

Vidit suum dulcem Natum
moriendo desolatum,
dum emisit spiritum.

STABAT MATER

At the Cross her station keeping,
stood the mournful Mother weeping,
close to Jesus to the last.

Through her heart, His sorrow sharing,
all His bitter anguish bearing,
now at length the sword has passed.

O how sad and sore distressed
was that Mother, highly blest,
of the sole-begotten One.

Christ above in torment hangs,
she beneath beholds the pangs
of her dying glorious Son.

Is there one who would not weep,
whelmed in miseries so deep,
Christ's dear Mother to behold?

Can the human heart refrain
from partaking in her pain,
in that Mother's pain untold?

Bruised, derided, cursed, defiled,
she beheld her tender Child
All with bloody scourges rent:

For the sins of His own nation,
saw Him hang in desolation,
Till His spirit forth He sent.

Time and the Temple

Eia, Mater, fons amoris
me sentire vim doloris
fac, ut tecum lugeam.

Fac, ut ardeat cor meum
in amando Christum Deum
ut sibi complaceam.

Sancta Mater, istud agas,
crucifixi fige plagas
cordi meo valide.

Tui Nati vulnerati,
tam dignati pro me pati,
poenas mecum divide.

Fac me tecum pie flere,
crucifixo condolere,
donec ego vixero.

Iuxta Crucem tecum stare,
et me tibi sociare
in planctu desidero.

Virgo virginum praeclara,
mihi iam non sis amara,
fac me tecum plangere.

Fac, ut portem Christi mortem,
passionis fac consortem,
et plagas recolere.

Fac me plagis vulnerari,
fac me Cruce inebriari,
et cruore Filii.

O thou Mother! fount of love!
Touch my spirit from above,
make my heart with thine accord:

Make me feel as thou hast felt;
make my soul to glow and melt
with the love of Christ my Lord.

Holy Mother! pierce me through,
in my heart each wound renew
of my Savior crucified:

Let me share with thee His pain,
who for all my sins was slain,
who for me in torments died.

Let me mingle tears with thee,
mourning Him who mourned for me,
all the days that I may live:

By the Cross with thee to stay,
there with thee to weep and pray,
is all I ask of thee to give.

Virgin of all virgins blest!,
Listen to my fond request:
let me share thy grief divine;

Let me, to my latest breath,
in my body bear the death
of that dying Son of thine.

Wounded with His every wound,
steep my soul till it hath swooned,
in His very Blood away;

Appendix

Flammis ne urar succensus,
per te, Virgo, sim defensus
in die iudicii.

Christe, cum sit hinc exire,
da per Matrem me venire
ad palmam victoriae.

Quando corpus morietur,
fac, ut animae donetur
paradisi gloria. Amen.

Be to me, O Virgin, nigh,
lest in flames I burn and die,
in His awful Judgment Day.

Christ, when Thou shalt call me hence,
by Thy Mother my defense,
by Thy Cross my victory;

While my body here decays,
may my soul Thy goodness praise,
safe in paradise with Thee. Amen.

Translation by Fr. Edward Caswall

TO THE BELOVED

By Giacomo Leopardi

Beauty beloved, who hast my heart inspired,
Seen from afar, or with thy face concealed,
Save, when in visions of the night revealed,
Or seen in daydreams bright,
When all the fields are filled with light,
And Nature's smile is sweet,
Say, hast thou blessed
Some golden age of innocence,
And floatest, now, a shadow, o'er the earth?
Or hath Fate's envious doom
Reserved thee for some happier day to come?
To see thee e'er alive,
No hope remains to me;
Unless perchance, when from this body free,
My wandering spirit, lone,
O'er some new path, to some new world hath flown.
E'en here, at first, I, at the dawn
Of this, my day, so dreary and forlorn,
Sought thee, to guide me on my weary way:
But none on earth resembles thee. E'en if
One were in looks and acts and words thy peer,
Though like thee, she less lovely would appear.

Amidst the deepest grief
That fate hath e'er to human lot assigned,
Could one but love thee on this earth,
Alive, and such as my thought painteth thee,
He would be happy in his misery:
And I most clearly see, how, still,
As in my earliest days,

Appendix

Thy love would make me cling to virtue's ways.
Unto my grief heaven hath no comfort brought;
And yet with thee, this mortal life would seem
Like that in heaven, of which we fondly dream.

Along the valleys where is heard
The song of the laborious husbandman,
And where I sit and moan
O'er youth's illusions gone;
Along the hills, where I recall with tears,
The vanished joys and hopes of earlier years,
At thought of thee, my heart revives again.
O could I still thy image dear retain,
In this dark age, and in this baleful air!
To loss of thee, O let me be resigned,
And in thy image still some comfort find!

If thou art one of those
Ideas eternal, which the Eternal Mind
Refused in earthly form to clothe,
Nor would subject unto the pain and strife
Of this, our frail and dreary life;
Or if thou hast a mansion fair,
Amid the boundless realms of space,
That lighted is by a more genial sun,
And breathest there a more benignant air;
From here, where brief and wretched are our days,
Receive thy humble lover's hymn of praise!

—*Translated by Frederick Townsend*

Notes

INTRODUCTION

1 In the juxtaposition of "temple" and "time," Giussani is making a play on words: in Italian, the two words differ only by a single letter (*tempio* and *tempo*). [Trans.]

2 By "positivity," Giussani refers to a meaning and purpose of goodness, rather than a good feeling—although awareness of the former does give rise to joy. Cf. Luigi Giussani, *Affezione e Dimora*, BUR, 2001. [Trans.]

3 Jacopone da Todi, "O novo canto," in *Laudi, trattato e detti*, edited by F. Ageno, Le monnier, 1953, verses 73-74, 264.

CHAPTER 1

4 In the experience of the *Memores Domini*, the "profession" is the lifelong commitment to adhere to those ideals in which the Church has traditionally located the realization of true humanity, that is, a humanity generated by the death and resurrection of Christ and continually renewed in baptism. The *Memores Domini* are those who live a dedication to Christ and to the Church in virginity. The experience was born in the movement of Communion and Liberation. The Association of the *Memores Domini* (commonly referred to as the "Adult Group") seeks to actualize a missionary presence precisely through the form of virginity in order to bring faith back into the lives of men and women, encountering them everywhere, but in particular in the various spheres of the working world: school, office, or factory. The *Memores Domini* tend to live together in "houses," in a companionship made up of three to twelve people.

5 Cf. Galatians 3:6-25. In verses 24-25, the word "disciplinarian" or "guardian" comes from the Greek *paidagōgos*, which refers to a slave with the duty of escorting and supervising boys but not teaching them directly. Saint Paul applies this image to the law of the people of Israel. [Trans.]

6 That is, the coming of Christ in history. The etymological root of the word

Notes

"event" is from the Latin *evenire*, which means "to come" or "to happen." This origin is clearer in the Italian ("event" = *avvenimento*, "to come" = *venire*), which helps account for Giussani's preference for it as a term for Christ's Incarnation. [Trans.]

7 "List" in Italian is *elenco* which comes from the Greek *élenkhos*, which refers to a proof, or that by which a thing is proved or tested. [Trans.]

8 Latin for "full of grace," as in Luke 1:28 and the Hail Mary. [Trans.]

9 The inscription is on the altar in the grotto under the Church of the Annunciation in Nazareth. Giussani refers to the pilgrim's vantage point as he or she descends the stairs from the church and thus looks down on the grotto. [Trans.]

10 A house of the *Memores Domini* was founded in Nazareth in 1994. [Trans.]

11 Giussani is referring to members of the *Memores Domini* who already made their professions and are thus "older companions" to the novices to whom he is primarily addressing his words. Novices, who are in a probationary period, live in houses with professed members while preparing for their own professions. Additionally, some professed *Memores Domini* are actively involved in forming novices, and therefore would have been present in the room during this address. [Trans.]

12 The demiurge is a figure in Platonic philosophy, an artisan responsible for shaping and maintaining the physical universe. [Trans.]

13 *Christe, cunctorum dominator alme* [Christ, the master of all things], the hymn for the dedication of a church [in the Ambrosian Breviary], *Analecta Hymnica Medii Aevi*, vol. 27, edited by C. Blume, Leipzig 1897, 265. The entire text can be found in the Appendix.

14 *Veni, Creator Spiritus* [Come, Creator Spirit] is a ninth-century hymn attributed to Rabanus Maurus and sung at Pentecost and other occasions associated with the descent of the Holy Spirit. [Trans.]

15 See note 6 on the use of the word "event." [Trans.]

16 This phrase refers to the tension between the universal salvific promise of the Church and its particular, historical realization through specific communities. While the mission of groups like the *Memores Domini* extends to all places ("Tibet is promised"), their specific, physical "dwelling place" has not yet been established there ("not yet chosen"). [Trans.]

17 Giussani commonly uses the word "I" to refer to the core of a person as an active subject who is responsible, free, and full of expectation. In this, he is drawing on the grammatical usage of "I" as a subject pronoun in contrast to "me" as an object pronoun. [Trans.]

18 Fr. Emmanuel Braghini (1928-2012) was a Capuchin friar from Brescia who became friends with Fr. Giussani as a young priest in the 1950s; years

Notes

later, he moved to Milan and collaborated with Fr. Giussani in educating young people, in addition to being very active as a confessor and spiritual director. [Trans.]

19 Mother Rosaria Spreafico, who from 1988 has been the abbess of the Trappistine Monastery of Our Lady of Saint Joseph in Vitorchiano, Italy. [Trans.]

20 The word "prophet" comes from the Greek *pro* (before or toward) and *phēmí* (to speak or say). [Trans.]

21 The entire text can be found in the Appendix. [Trans.]

22 "... but my life / Like a cold and burning March day / Unadorned and fruitful, without ceasing / Brightens and darkens, burns and is overshadowed / With contentment and disdainful peace ..." (From Maria Barbara Tosatti, "Resurrezione," *Canti e Preghiere* [Songs and Prayers], Morcelliana, Brescia 1945, 29-30. Translation mine. [Trans.]

23 Luigi Giussani, *Why the Church?*, McGill-Queen's University Press, 2001, 222-223.

24 This phrase, from the second Canto of Dante Alighieri's *Inferno*, translates to: "Here your nobility will be manifest!" [Trans.]

25 Luigi Giussani, *Is It Possible to Live This Way? An Unusual Approach to Christian Existence, Volume 1: Faith*, McGill-Queen's University Press, 2008.

26 Cf. O.V. Milosz, *Miguel Mañara*, Jaca Book, 1976, 63. See note 76.

27 See the article by Carmine di Martino, *He is if He Changes: Notes from conversations with young people. August 1992 - September 1993*. Introduction by Cardinal Jean-Jérôme Hamer. Supplement to *30 Days*, 7-8 (1994). [Trans.]

28 Luigi Giussani, *Is It Possible to Live This Way?* Volume 3, Charity. McGill-Queen's University Press, 2009.

29 Luigi Giussani, *He Is If He Changes: Notes from conversations with young people. August 1992 - September 1993.*

30 A fresco created by the Dominican friar Guido di Pietro, also called Fra Angelico, in 1440-1441 in a cell of his priory at San Marco, Florence. The painting depicts the encounter between Mary Magdalene and the risen Christ described in John 20. [Trans.]

31 For Giussani, virginity is not the absence of loving relationship with another, but its truest form. He distinguishes between "true possession" (which is affirming the other's destiny and relationship with the Mystery) and "grasping" (which is instinctively trying to seize the other person for oneself). True possession requires an inner "distance" or "detachment," which gives space for respect and imitates God's own gratuitous love. Thus,

Notes

"restraint" is the condition for a love that is total; without it, one grasps and reduces the other to an object. See Luigi Giussani, *Is It Possible to Live This Way? Vol. 3: Charity* (Montreal: McGill-Queen's University Press, 2009) and *All Things: Mystery and Sign* (*Traces*, 1999). For a profound exposition of Giussani's understanding of virginity, including its connection to the *Noli me tangere*, see Paolo Prosperi, "Do Not Hold Me: Ascending the Ladder of Love," *Communio* 45 (Summer 2018). [Trans.]

32 Cf. Saint Augustine, *De libero arbitrio*, III, ch. 9; *De gestis Pelagii*, XIV, ch. 36; *Epistola* 131.

33 T.S. Eliot, *The Complete Poems and Plays* (Harcourt Brace Jovanovich, 1950), 281.

34 The letter uses the formal form of second-person pronouns and verbs, despite the informal greeting and the familiarity with which the author writes. [Trans.]

35 Luigi Giussani, *The Religious Sense*, New revised edition, McGill-Queen's University Press, 2023.

36 Marco Zibardi, a *Memor Domini* who graduated in 1987 from Allende High School in Milan with the author of the letter. [Trans.]

37 Cf. Thomas Aquinas, *Summa Theologiae*, II, IIae, q. 179, a. 1, *Respondeo*: "Unde etiam in hominibus vita uniuscuiusque hominis videtur esse id in quo maxime delectatur et cui maxime intendit."

38 This letter was published in "*Litterae Communionis-Tracce*" n. 11, December 1994, 4.

CHAPTER 2

39 "There is a goal, but no way"—from Franz Kafka, *Il silenzio delle sirene. Scritti e frammenti postumi* (1917–1924), Feltrinelli, 1994, 91.

40 "Unknown land" in Latin. [Trans.]

41 An ancient European tribe that lived in Jutland in the fourth century BC and that fought the Romans in France in the second century BC. [Trans.]

42 Tacitus, *Germania*, IX, 2.

43 Giovanni Battista Cardinal Montini, the future Saint Paul VI, was archbishop of Milan from 1954 until his election as Pope in 1963 and was known for his ecumenical relations with other Christian denominations and non-Christian religions. [Trans.]

44 Luigi Giussani, *At the Origin of the Christian Claim*, New revised edition, McGill-Queen's University Press, 2026.

45 "I had before my eyes the darkness. The abyss / That has no shore and no summit / Was there, bleak, immense; and nothing stirred. / I felt lost in

the mute inferno. / Deep down, through the shadow, impenetrable veil, / God could be seen like a dark star. / I cried out—My soul, o my soul! It would be necessary / To cross this abyss where no shore appears, / And for you to walk through this night to your God, / To build a giant bridge over millions of arches. / Who could ever do it? No one can! O mourning! Dread! / Grief!—A white ghost stood before me / As I cast an eye of alarm over the shadow, / And this ghost had the shape of a tear; / It was a virgin's brow with the hands of a child; / It resembled the lily that its whiteness defended; / Its hands, in joining, made light. / It showed me the abyss where all dust goes, / So profound that no echo ever answers it, / And said to me: If you want, I will build the bridge. / Toward this pale stranger I raised my eyelids. / What is your name? I said to him. He told me: Prayer." (Victor Hugo, "Le Pont," in *Les Contemplations*, Michel Lévy Frères-Hetzel-Pagnerre, 1857). [Translation SC]

46 Latin for "there is no third option," the axiom that either a proposition or its negation is true. [Trans.]

47 *Pondus* is Latin for heavy and firm. [Trans.]

48 Luigi Giussani, *The Religious Sense*.

49 Cf. Thomas Aquinas, *Summa Theologiae*, II, IIae, q. 179, a. 1, *Respondeo*: "Unde etiam in hominibus vita uniuscuiusque hominis videtur esse id in quo maxime delectatur et cui maxime intendit."

50 This letter was published in *"Litterae Communionis-Tracce"* n. 11, December 1994, 4.

51 See *He Is If He Changes: Notes from conversations with young people. August 1992 - September 1993.* [Trans.]

52 *Traces* is the international magazine of the movement of Communion and Liberation, which shares stories of Christian witness and perspectives on current events throughout the world. [Trans.]

53 The reference is to severe flooding in the fall of 1994 that hit the Piedmont region of Italy in particular.

54 "O Cristo o niente" ["Either Christ or Nothing"], *Litterae Communionis-Tracce*, December 1994, 11.

55 Bishop Massimo Camisasca is bishop emeritus of the Diocese of Reggio Emilia. In 1985, then-Fr. Massimo Camisasca founded the Priestly Fraternity of Missionaries of Saint Charles Borromeo, which draws its inspiration from the person and charism of Fr. Luigi Giussani. [Trans.]

56 Josif, "Dio è diventato avvenimento nella nostra vita" ["God Has Become an Event in our Life"], *Litterae Communionis-Tracce*, November 1994, 19.

57 Cf. *Il Sabato*, no. 5, 1 February 1986, 8.

58 Cf. *Il Sabato*, no. 22, 30 May 1987, 4.

Notes

59 The whole letter is published in *Litterae Communionis-Tracce*, n. 10, November 1994, 2-3.

60 Cf. D. Rondoni, "Edimàr, occhi e sangue" ["Edimàr, Eyes and Blood"], *Litterae Communionis-Tracce*, September 1994, 28-30.

61 Villa Turro is a clinic for patients with infectious diseases associated with the San Raffaele Hospital in Milan. [Trans.]

62 Giussani, *The Religious Sense*, 105-114. [Trans.]

63 "I have not lost you. You have remained, at the depths / of being. You are yourself yet another you are: / without frond or flower, without the shining / laughter you had in the time that does not return, / without that song. You are another, more beautiful. / You love, and think not to be loved: for every / flower that blossoms or fruit that blushes / or child that is born, to the God of the fields / and the generations you give thanks in your heart. / Year by year, within yourself, you changed / face and substance. Every sorrow more steadfast / made you: against every trace of the passing / of days, you put up as shelter / your hidden and green sap. Now you look to the Light / that does not deceive: in its mirror you gaze upon / life that endures. And you have remained / like an age that has no name: human / among the human miseries, and yet living / of God alone and only happy in him. / O timeless youth, o ever / renewed hope, I entrust you / to those who will come next: that at last on earth / spring may return to bloom, and in the heavens / the stars may rise when the sun has gone out." (A. Negri, "Mia Giovinezza" ["My Youth"] in *Mia giovinezza*, Bur, Milan, 2010, 78.) [Translation SC]

64 Noberto Bobbio was an Italian philosopher of law and political science who wrote regularly for the prominent newspaper *La Stampa*. [Trans.] N. Bobbio, "Gli dei che hanno fallito. Alcune domande sul problema del male," in *Elogio della mitezza e altri scritti morali*, ["The Gods Who Have Failed. Some Questions on the Problem of Evil," in *In Praise of Humility and Other Moral Writings*], Linea d'Ombra, 1994.

65 Giacomo Leopardi (1798–1837) was an Italian Romantic poet and philosopher. Giussani discovered his work during his early years in seminary, and heard in the poet's search for the infinite a profound echo of his own Christian experience—so much so that he memorized all of Leopardi's *Canti*. Throughout his life, Giussani referenced Leopardi as one who articulated the religious sense, even if Leopardi did not reach its fulfillment in faith. [Trans.]

66 See the Appendix for the full text of this poem, which is sometimes translated as "To His Lady."

67 Luigi Giussani, *Why the Church?*, McGill-Queen's University Press, 2001, 222-223.

Notes

CHAPTER 3

68 The "Easter poster" is a text for meditation accompanied by an image that, every year from 1982, the Movement of Communion and Liberation has printed and distributed on the occasion of the Sacred Triduum.

69 "And the Spirit moved upon the face of the water. / And men who turned towards the light and were known of the light / Invented the Higher Religions; and the Higher Religions were good / And led men from light to light, to knowledge of God and Evil. / But their light was ever surrounded and shot with darkness / As the air of temperate seas is pierced by the still dead breath of the Arctic Current; / And they came to an end, a dead end stirred with a flicker of life, / And they came to the withered ancient look of a child that has died of starvation. / Prayer wheels, worship of the dead, denial of this world, affirmation of rites with forgotten meanings / In the restless wind-whipped sand, or the hills where the wind will not let the snow rest. / Waste and void. Waste and void. And darkness on the face of the deep." (T.S. Eliot, *The Rock*, VII, Houghton Mifflin Harcourt, 2014.)

70 *Memor Domini* is Latin for "mindful of the Lord" or "those who remember the Lord." [Trans.]

71 Jacopone da Todi, "O novo canto," in *Laudi, trattati e detti*, a cura di F. Ageno, Le monnier, 1953, verses 73-74, 264

72 Jacopone da Todi, *Stabat Mater*, verses 28-30. The whole text is available in the Appendix.

73 The reference is to the year in which Muhammad fled Mecca for Medina, marking the beginning of the Islamic age. [Trans.]

74 The author is alluding to a scene from Oscar Milosz's play *Miguel Mañara*, in which an abbot tells the weeping protagonist that his past sins "never existed" because they were not simply pardoned but obliterated by the totalizing power of Christ's mercy. [Trans.]

75 S. Kierkegaard, *Diario del seduttore*, Newton Compton, 1993, 75.

76 Msgr. Eugenio Corecco was the bishop of Lugano and a friend of Fr. Giussani, along with Pope Saint John Paul II and Pope Benedict XVI. This exchange occurred in January 1994, as he was suffering from cancer. Msgr. Corecco died in March 1995, shortly before Giussani gave this meditation. [Trans.]

77 P.B. Shelley, "To a Skylark," vv. 86–87.

78 "For the Christians are distinguished from other men neither by country, nor language, nor the customs which they observe. For they neither inhabit cities of their own, nor employ a peculiar form of speech, nor lead a life which is marked out by any singularity. The course of conduct which they follow has not been devised by any speculation or deliberation of inquisitive men; nor do they, like some, proclaim themselves the advocates

Notes

of any merely human doctrines. But, inhabiting Greek as well as barbarian cities, according as the lot of each of them has determined, and following the customs of the natives in respect to clothing, food, and the rest of their ordinary conduct, they display to us their wonderful and confessedly striking method of life. They dwell in their own countries, but simply as sojourners. As citizens, they share in all things with others, and yet endure all things as if foreigners. Every foreign land is to them as their native country, and every land of their birth as a land of strangers. They marry, as do all; they beget children; but they do not destroy their offspring. They have a common table, but not a common bed. They are in the flesh, but they do not live after the flesh. They pass their days on earth, but they are citizens of heaven. They obey the prescribed laws, and at the same time surpass the laws by their lives. They love all men, and are persecuted by all. They are unknown and condemned; they are put to death, and restored to life. They are poor, yet make many rich; they are in lack of all things, and yet abound in all; they are dishonoured, and yet in their very dishonour are glorified. They are evil spoken of, and yet are justified; they are reviled, and bless; they are insulted, and repay the insult with honour; they do good, yet are punished as evil-doers. When punished, they rejoice as if quickened into life; they are assailed by the Jews as foreigners, and are persecuted by the Greeks; yet those who hate them are unable to assign any reason for their hatred." *Letter to Diognetus*, ch. 5. Translated by Alexander Roberts and James Donaldson. From *Ante-Nicene Fathers*, Vol. 1. Edited by Alexander Roberts, James Donaldson, and A. Cleveland Coxe. (Christian Literature Publishing Co., 1885.)

79 *Detti e fatti dei Padri del deserto* [*Sayings and Deeds of the Desert Fathers*], Rusconi, 1975, 118.

80 The Italian word translated as "reluctance" is *reticenza* from the Latin *reticere*, which means "to be silent." Here, Giussani is indicating that the core of one's resistance to Christ lies in withholding—keeping silent about both the "no" of one's doubts and the answering "yes" of abandonment to Christ. The problem is a skeptical, lukewarm "maybe" about one's vocation. See Revelation 3:14-16. [Trans.]

81 "The lost good: / a brief rocket fallen in tears. / What I had grasped, longing, / in my clenched hands fell apart, / like the rose in the evening / under the vault of eternity. / Everything paled, fell silent, / lost color and flavor, / (and most of all that which I liked most). / However, terrified by fear / of losing again the gift that does not last, / I renounced happiness / but one happiness / yet remains for me to ask of Thee, Lord, / One at which you aim / for the elect of your love: / that—yes—of singing in martyrdom." (O. Mazzoni, *Noi peccatori: liriche* 1883-1936, Zanichelli 1930, 72). [Translation SC]

82 Saint Augustine, *De civitate Dei*, XIX, 24.

Notes

83 This Latin root of the word "intuit" refers to "looking at" or "contemplating." [Trans.]

84 *Detti e fatti*, 99.

85 Irenaeus, *Adversus Haereses*. 4.20.7, trans. Robert M. Grant, *Irenaeus of Lyons*.

CHAPTER 4

86 From the hymn *Christe, cunctorum dominator alme*. The whole text is available in the Appendix.

87 A weekly meeting held in every house of the *Memores Domini*. [Trans.]

88 The previous three chapters of this text. [Trans.]

89 Cf. O.V. *Miguel Mañara*, 63. See note 74.

90 *Didachè*, IV, 2, in *I padri apostolici*, Città Nuova editrice, 1978, 32.

91 Giovanni Maspes was a *Memor Domini* who went on mission to Moscow in 1994, writing a letter a few months later to the friends he had left behind in Italy, with the phrase: "When I stepped onto that airplane on 19 July I understood that it was a definitive choice, for eternity. Not eternity as the extension of time, but eternity as the depth of the instant." The words captivated Giussani, who repeatedly reflected on them in his subsequent speeches. See Ch. 30 of Alberto Savorana, *The Life of Luigi Giussani*, McGill-Queen's University Press, 2017. [Trans.]

92 "For us men," from the Nicene Creed. [Trans.]

93 Augustine, *Sermo* 34.1-3, 5-6; CCL 41, 424-426.

94 Ephrem the Syrian, sections 3-4 and 9 of the Eastertide sermon "On Our Lord."

95 Cf. *Detti e fatti dei Padri del deserto* [*Sayings and Deeds of the Desert Fathers*], op. cit., 69.

96 The Spiritual Exercises of the Fraternity of Communion and Liberation are an annual educational moment of prayer and reflection on a particular theme of the Christian life. [Trans.]

97 In Homer's epic poem *The Odyssey*, Odysseus uses the name "Nobody" to trick and escape from the Cyclops Polyphemus. [Trans.]

98 Etymologically, from Latin, the word originally referred to a guardian deity or spirit that indicated the nature of a person or a place. [Trans.]

99 Cf. Maria Barbara Tosatti, "Resurrezione," *Canti e Preghiere* [*Songs and Prayers*], Morcelliana, 1945, 29-30. See note 22 of this text.

100 Etymologically, "nostalgia" comes from the Greek *nostos* (to return home) and *algos* (pain) and thus indicates an acute homesickness. [Trans.]

Notes

101 O.V. Milosz, *Miguel Mañara*, 63. See note 74.
102 The "School of Community" refers to the weekly catechetical meeting of the movement of Communion and Liberation. [Trans.]
103 That is, the request to get to know and participate in the movement of Communion and Liberation. [Trans.]
104 Colossians 1:17. The Greek word often translated into English as "hold together," *synestēken*, literally means "to consist of." [Trans.]
105 The Italian word for "understand," *capire* comes from the Latin *capere*, to seize, grasp, or hold. In English, the most closely related words are "capture" and "catch." With a similar meaning but distinct root, "comprehend" comes from the Latin *com* (together) and *prehendere* (to grasp). [Trans.]

This book was set in Adobe Caslon Pro, designed by Carol Twombly and released in 1990. The typeface is named after the British typefounder William Caslon (1692–1766) and grew out of Twombly's study of Caslon's specimen sheets produced between 1734 and 1770. Though Caslon began his career making "exotic" typefaces—Hebrew, Arabic, and Coptic—his Roman typeface became the standard for text printed in English for most of the eighteenth century, including the Declaration of Independence.

This book was designed by Shannon Carter, Ian Creeger, and Gregory Wolfe. It was published in hardcover, paperback, and electronic formats by Slant Books, Seattle, Washington.

Cover art: Georges Rouault, *Paysage biblique*, circa 1949. © 2026 Artists Rights Society (ARS), New York / ADAGP, Paris.

www.ingramcontent.com/pod-product-compliance
Lightning Source LLC
Chambersburg PA
CBHW032235080426
42735CB00008B/861